Adapting to the End of Oil

Adapting to the End of Oil

Toward an Earth-Centered Spirituality

Maynard Kaufman

To order additional copies of this book, contact:
Xlibris Corporation
1-888-795-4274
www.Xlibris.com
Orders@Xlibris.com
51768

Contents

Introduction 9

PART ONE

Chapter I.   A Nation In Denial About Oil 19

Chapter II.   Cultural Roots of Our Denial of Limits 35

Chapter III.   Changes Needed As We Adapt To The End of Oil 53

Chapter IV.   Interlude: Gazing Into A Crystal Ball 79

PART TWO

Religion and Spirituality After Oil

Chapter V.   Maladaptive Elements In Christianity 93

Chapter VI.   Problems And Possibilities With End-Time Anxiety 102

Chapter VII.   Earth-Centered Emphasis In Recent Religious Thought.... 109

Chapter VIII.   Recovery Of Earth-Based Spirituality 119

Chapter IX.   Navigating The Currents of Cultural Change 137

Endnotes.. 149

Bibliography 161

DEDICATION

This book is dedicated to my wife Barbara for her critical insights as First Reader

And also to Michele and Don for their work on the cover; to Ken for his academic critique and encouragement; to Bobbi, Carol and Nancy, the helpful women in the library; to Jon, for his patient help with computer problems; to Paul, for helping me express myself; and to all the writers and activists who try to awaken Americans to the urgency of peak oil and climate change.

INTRODUCTION

Until recently most of us were unaware of the fact that our civilization was made possible by burning oil. Although a few environmentalists worried about the pollution caused by burning oil, most of us took oil for granted and enjoyed the easy life it made possible. Even now, as more people are aware that burning oil leads to global warming, and that the rate of global oil production is about to peak, few recognize the uniqueness of our time, that the age of oil is an anomaly in human history. This bonanza of cheap energy never happened before and will very likely never happen again. Most of the oil will have been used in about a century, from about 1930 to 2030, and a large proportion of this oil was burned by Americans. The United States, with less than 5% of the world's population, continues to use at least 25% of its oil. Thus the end of oil is an American problem. This book asks how Americans can adapt to having less when their personal experience and cultural history have always provided them with more and the promise of still more. We have evolved a way of life that is increasingly dependent on shrinking petroleum reserves, and our dependency has led to serious problems.

The first problem is that the burning of fossil fuels is a major contribution to global warming as more carbon dioxide accumulates in the atmosphere and creates a greenhouse effect. It seems increasingly certain that this warming of the atmosphere will lead to climate change on the planet. The results are not fully known; there may be some winners and some losers in the process. The effects of global warming could be disastrous and make it imperative that people on the planet should cut back on the burning of oil and other fossil fuels, such as gas and especially coal, which is the most polluting. We must therefore adapt to the end of oil for two reasons: because the demand will soon exceed the supply and because burning the remaining oil will damage the planet.

The second reason why it is prudent to adapt to the end of oil is that those nations that refuse to adapt seem ready to make war to get more than their share.

It has been the strategy of the United States to be in military control of oil-rich areas in the Middle East. This was made clear as a policy by President Carter during the OPEC (Organization of Petroleum Exporting Countries) oil embargo during the 1970s and acted out by both the first and the second President Bush as they invaded Iraq. Although a large majority of Americans by 2008 opposed the continuation of the war in Iraq, few seem fully aware of how it relates to our dependence on oil—perhaps because our government has denied that it is a war for oil.

The third reason why it would be good for us to affirm the end of oil is that the basis of our civilization is shifting. The enormous amount of oil that was available enabled the development of an industrial civilization that has replaced agrarian societies for about half of the people in the world. Where oil was available it gradually obliterated pre-industrial modes of production. Our food is produced with oil, our transportation is provided with oil-burning machines, and our homes are heated with oil or other fossil fuels such as natural gas or coal. All this will change when the supply of oil can no longer keep pace with demand and prices rise dramatically. But because such fundamental change is unprecedented, most Americans are still in denial. At best they may seek technological solutions and substitutes for oil that would prolong industrial civilization, while refusing to recognize the need for a deeper moral reorientation. This book will clarify the values that shape American technological optimism and the exuberance that expects more affluence. In the second part of the book I suggest examples of earth-centered spirituality that could help us adapt to the coming era of expensive oil and a post-industrial civilization.

I should be clear at the outset that I am using the word "adapting" in the title in both its active and passive senses. Certainly it is necessary that we must reexamine our religious traditions and values so that we can adjust to changing circumstances. Thus we adapt. But it is also necessary to make real changes in the real world, actually adapt our world, to the decline in energy resources. For example, our reliance on the automobile for most of our transportation will have to be changed. Some technological down-sizing might be in order. We already have some religious and cultural resources that can help us make these changes, and more are emerging as new options. Since the energy crisis of the 1970s, we also have a significant body of literature that can help us understand what must be done on the practical levels of economics and technology.

Older readers who remember the energy crisis of the 1970s may feel they have been through all this already. Even then the oil embargo by OPEC (Organization of Petroleum Exporting Countries) succeeded because oil production had peaked in the United States early in the 1970s. This should have been a wake-up call to Americans, but conservation efforts during the Carter administration, along with new discoveries stimulated by higher prices, provided for surplus oil and, eventually, cheaper energy prices. People were glad to assume that the energy crisis was over. There was quite literally a counter-revolution presided over by Ronald Reagan as he had the solar panels on the White House roof taken down and junked. If social responses to the energy crisis of the 1970s are precedents for what we can expect now, thirty years later, there will be little planning for alternatives as oil production peaks.

Concern over environmental quality became widespread as the decade of the 1970s began. As a young professor at Western Michigan University, I was caught up in this concern and served on the committee that organized the Environmental Studies Program and its curriculum. Like many others during that time I had purchased a small farm to live on and my wife and children and I enjoyed raising our food. It soon became obvious, thanks to Rachel Carson's book on the effects of pesticides, that organic methods of farming and gardening that do not depend on chemical pesticides and fertilizers could help in preserving environmental quality and human health. As a result I became active in organic farming organizations and helped with the forming of Organic Growers of Michigan and Michigan Land Trustees. Later I organized Michigan Organic Food and Farm Alliance and functioned as a leader in the organic movement in Michigan.

As an environmentalist I was also aware of the pollution caused by the burning of fossil fuels and that supplies of oil were limited. At one point, in about 1971 or 1972, I was invited to an important academic conference on religion and ecology in California and my university provided my airline ticket. But as I thought about the environmental impact of flying that far, I decided not to go. Some of my colleagues thought this was problematic, along with the way I failed to exploit my vertically-mobile teaching career. Instead of accepting the chair of the department when it was offered, I decided to start a homesteading program. Feeling the need for an educational program that would offer training in frugal and low-energy living, I sought and received a half-time leave of absence from classroom teaching to develop a "School of Homesteading" on my farm. We had about eight students in residence for an eight-month term each growing season. Among other reasons, my wife and I started this venture because we felt that a time of scarcity was at hand and that household food production and preservation was not just conducive to environmental quality but guaranteed personal survival. Needless to say, many other people felt that way as they participated in the back-to-the-land movement of the 1970s. We may have been a bit precocious, ahead of the times, but given the lead time needed to move from a global to local food systems, we would all be better off today if the homesteading movement of the seventies had continued as vigorously as it began.

Unfortunately, this movement lost its vigor in the 1980s; what could have been a sustained practical effort generating its own intellectual rationale was removed to remote cultural margins. This marginalization meant that millions of young people grew up with hardly a hint of a more realistic long-term assessment of our energy predicament and with little or no understanding of hands-on practical ways in which this predicament might be met.

Because Americans still exhibit considerable ignorance of ecology and of their place in nature, it is absolutely essential that the religious or spiritual orientation that might help people adapt to lower energy use should not only be congruent with ecology and evolution, but reinforce the insights they provide. A change in energy supply will be a major cultural shift for which a new spiritual matrix is needed to move us past inertia and denial.

The first chapter of this book will provide a perspective on the current energy crisis by comparing it to the energy crisis of thirty years ago. The response of Americans to that crisis, essentially one of denial, seems also to be the response to the current energy crisis. The shortage of oil in the 1970s seemed to be a false alarm, so why worry? Now, as the symptoms of climate change or global warming become more dramatic, it is reasonable to hope that more nations will voluntarily curtail the use of oil even before it is all gone.

We can also gain a perspective on the peak oil phenomenon by reviewing how the development of technology that was able to harness oil enlarged the carrying capacity of the planet. (Carrying capacity refers to populations that do not exceed limiting factors.) This is a very difficult topic for most Americans because they prefer to think in economic rather than in ecological terms. It is easy to be proud of our technological achievements, especially in agriculture, which allowed the global population to grow from one billion in around 1800 to two billion in 1930, to three billion in 1960, to four billion in 1974, to five billion in 1987 and to six billion in 1999. Obviously this kind of growth in population cannot continue for much longer, given the ecological stress it places on our planet. The Four Horsemen of the Apocalypse are waiting in the wings, ready to ride. The enlargement of carrying capacity may turn out to be a tragic illusion. It was oil that made this increase possible and we will learn to recognize the fossil fuel era as an anomalous and tragic period in human history. Without cheap oil the earth will not be able to support its human population—certainly not without a reversal of direction by the world's remaining empire (the U. S. A.) as it is impoverishing most of its subjects.

The second chapter draws on my academic background in the study of religion and culture. The Jewish and Christian traditions have been anthropocentric and Christianity has been contaminated by empire. In the Creation myth we see an entire world created for humans who are given dominion over it. Sacred history evolved as a religious form more important than the sacredness of nature. History was seen as the history of salvation. As the idea of Divine Providence took more secular forms it was transformed into the ideology of progress. This was reinforced in this country by the plentitude experienced by those who invaded and settled here. Resources seemed to be limitless, especially after we eliminated most of the indigenous peoples. Anything was possible. We became a "culture of exuberance" as William Catton put it in his book *Overshoot*. Economic growth was seen as progress, or, to put it another way, progress was mechanized by economic growth and measured by the gross domestic product. The refusal to acknowledge limits can be understood as a demonic presence in our society, illustrated by the Faust legend and embodied most fully in today's gigantic business corporations. These religious and cultural traditions will make it very difficult for people to accept "limits to growth", and they must be clearly understood if we are to avoid social collapse.

The third chapter explores the changes needed as we move toward a post-petroleum society. Most of the needed changes are on a practical level, shifts that can move us toward a sustainable way of life. The changes will add up to a paradigm shift from an economic to an ecological paradigm in our society. We can also understand these competing paradigms as dominant and recessive genes in our cultural organism. Aside from the chapters on religious adaptations in Part Two, this chapter is the most important one in the book, and the longest.

The fourth chapter is a more imaginative interlude which takes a look into the future Many of the changes that will be necessary at the time of the end of oil will restore true meaning that was lost as we became an affluent society and sought fulfillment in consumerism. There are some socially desirable aspects to the end of oil—along with risks.

Part Two will explore religious and spiritual adaptations to the post-petroleum reality. It begins with a chapter listing some of the dysfunctional elements in Christianity as it has evolved in our time under the aegis of global empire. As the economic basis of our lives changes with the end of cheap oil, it is crucial that some elements of Christianity be reformed or abandoned if we are to have social harmony. These elements include patriarchal modes of thought and behaviour, expectations of continuing progress, traditional notions of sin and salvation which distract us from the splendor of creation, and the dangers of confusing myth and science in the thinking of the Religious Right, especially in relation to ecology and politics.

Since this book argues that we will be moving into a future that will be radically different from the past, I am suggesting that this move must be supported by new forms of spirituality which open new cultural possibilities. Christianity, as it evolved with Western civilization, has not been supportive of an ecological way of life. Also, while I do not question the goodness of the historical Jesus, the peasant who has been rediscovered by scholars such as John Dominic Crossan, (1) the religion Jesus started soon evolved to betray the Kingdom he promised. For example, Jim Wallis (2) has reminded us that Jesus and the Bible are most concerned about the poor. But where are the Christian churches on this issue? Very few oppose the corporations for stealing from the poor around the world.

There are, of course, many texts in the Jewish and Christian scriptures that celebrate the glory of the created world, and there are increasing numbers of Christian ecological thinkers and writers, including Evangelical Christians who have recently emphasized "Creation Care." But, taken as a whole religion/ culture complex, Christianity, especially as it has affirmed industrial technology and corporate capitalism, has done more damage to the earth than any other of the great religions. So I am describing and calling for an earth-centered spirituality.

I want to be clear about the term "earth-centered" and what it implies. First, it is not anti-Christian although it does support a move beyond Christianity. Second, it seeks and finds the locus of the Divine Presence in nature more than in history. Third, an earth-centered spirituality is possible on a theological level as a theology of the Third Person of the Trinity. (Early Christian thinkers saw fit to speak of one God manifest in three persons: Father, Son and Holy Spirit). In the confessions of Western Christianity the Holy Spirit is said to proceed from the Father and the Son, so that the Spiritual Presence is shaped by masculine divine beings and channeled through the Church. In Eastern Orthodoxy, which split from Western Christianity over this issue, the Son and the Spirit both proceed from the Father and as a result it has a richer sense for the divine in nature and in culture outside of Christianity. In ancient Hebrew tradition the spirit was symbolized by breath, or wind, a fitting natural symbol for life and vitality.

It is this recognition of the sacredness of nature that feminist thinkers have rediscovered, and in our time it is feminist religious thinkers who hold all the winning cards. It is tragic that patriarchal Christianity has discouraged their full participation and leadership. Since the Holy Spirit is related to Wisdom or Sophia, and is present in Mother Earth, it (She?) must be recognized as an independent divine reality. In effect Christianity has been a "Christocentric Unitarianism" of the Second Person, but in substantial sectors of religious culture we are now moving beyond it to a recognition of the free and creative presence of the Holy Spirit in nature, moving toward an earth-centered spirituality. Among contemporary religious thinkers Leonardo Boff has articulated these ideas. Also of value are books by theologians such as Rosemary Ruether and Mark I. Wallace, who argue for the relevance of a new emphasis on the Holy Spirit in relation to ecology, and include the witness of neo-pagans along with Christians.

Chapter VI will examine the likelihood that if the end of oil is experienced as the end of the world as we know it, there will be widespread cultural eruptions of apocalyptic or end-time anxiety. These can take destructive forms such as are already evident in the Religious Right. For example, what happens to society when those who already expect the second coming of Christ realize that the world as we know it is actually ending because of the end of oil or global warming? Some might welcome these events and resist those who advocate policies to mitigate global warming On the other hand, since the religious imagination in these circumstances postulates the rebirth of a new earth after the end of the old world, there are also very positive dynamics of social change inherent in end-time anxiety which could facilitate both spiritual and cultural transformation.

The emerging spiritual possibilities are discussed in two chapters that explain how they can be very helpful in a post-petroleum age. Chapter VII deals with creation-centered religious thinkers who very explicitly help us to think more ecologically. These forms of earth-centered spirituality may range from the Christian versions of Matthew Fox ("Creation Sprirituality"), to Thomas Berry, and to ecofeminism with its new ways of thinking about god and goddess. All are earth-centered to the extent that they no longer make sin and salvation central in spiritual experience. All are compatible with a panentheistic or process theology which affirms that "the world is God's body" or, as feminist religious thinkers might put it, the body of the goddess. All celebrate the blessings of the natural order or the wisdom of Mother Earth in judgment of her children. It is essential that the religious orientation for an age of scarcity should help people avoid blame and scapegoating and foster an attitude of acceptance of the great changes that are our fate.

The chapter on Earth-based spirituality begins with an attempt to outline its components. The argument will be made that a spiritual orientation such as that articulated by many eco-feminist thinkers would be the most useful in helping people adapt to life in a post-petroleum world. A more particular example is neo-paganism, already a rapidly growing spiritual orientation, even in our urban society. Without cheap oil vastly more people will be raising food; they will be living on the land in a most intimate way. The word "pagan" originally referred to people who dwell on the land. Virtually all pagans, past and present, celebrate the cycle of the seasons. Their orientation is cyclical rather than linear. They have neither a salvation history nor the personal experience of sin and salvation. They are reconciled to and integrated with the here and now in the natural world. The spiritual outlook of native Americans will also be relevant in new ways to the larger culture. These First Nations can teach us a great deal about living on the land in sustainable ways. All these aspects of earth religion are recessive genes in our cultural organism, and they had been repressed by the dominant genes, but we are now seeing the return of the repressed.

Examples of such paganism will be provided from various writers with special reference to Starhawk whose recent book, *The Earth Path*, most adequately fulfills the conditions set forth above. Her book is sub-titled "Grounding your Spirit in the Rhythms of Nature," and it most fully articulates the sacredness of ecology and what she calls "Gaian evolution". She provides rituals and information that enable the production of local organic food and renewable energy, along with a political activism that opposes corporate malfeasance such as the attempt to monopolize seeds or pollute the earth with genetically-modified organisms. Although, like many other neo-pagans, she refers to herself as a "witch" and writes about the use of magic, she uses magic to raise power during celebratory rituals and not as a technique to get power over nature or others. She is a healer in the old way, helping people become strong. But she is not a healer in that New Age sense where healing becomes a secular version of Christian salvation, detached from the reality of our earth home. She is insistent that wicca, or neo-paganism, must help people understand and respect science, especially ecology and evolution. This is really crucial now as so many religious people disregard science, and it will be ever more important as we enter the age of scarcity.

The final chapter explores the possibility of a shift from an economic to an ecological paradigm. Although the end of cheap oil may lead to scarcity and the threat of fascism, it may also serve to discredit the econocentric way of life and perhaps lead to the end of corporate hegemony, especially as more and more people are impoverished. A revitalization movement is not unlikely as many people suffer deprivation. The ethos of economic growth may give way to an emphasis on steady-state economics. A more austere economy, with more non-monetized activity, may replace the socially destructive functions of a voracious market economy. As we learn to live with much less, we may discover that the love of money was indeed the root of all evil. Above all, we may once again find, along with the challenges of adaptation to scarcity, a rich and fulfilling life as we are reintegrated with the rhythms of nature.

Some readers, especially those who will be introduced to the effects and challenges of the end of oil for the first time, may be upset by what they read in the following pages. Please don't shoot the messenger who bears bad news; all of us must face the fact that the end of oil may eventually lead to the end of industrial civilization, which is all most of us know. The continued burning of fossil fuels may lead to a less hospitable planet as it changes the climate—most likely during this 21st century. Finally, in the very near future the economic impact of high oil prices will likely trigger more resource wars such as we already see in Iraq and even more economic impoverishment in this country. Desperate political and military conflicts, between people who have nothing to lose, could even lead to nuclear war.

"May you live in interesting times" was said to be an ancient Chinese curse. We may be living through tragic times with the possibility of large die-offs in the human community. The damage that burning oil and gas has done to the earth may lead to more suffering and death. But the loss of the good things that fossil fuels have made possible for many people in the world is also tragic. In spite of the damage that fossil fuels have done, the twentieth century will surely be remembered as a time of great blessings.

This book is offered in the hope that it can add to the many voices already calling on Americans, the most profligate users of energy in the world, to look for ways to adapt to the end of oil. While this book may be depressing and upsetting to some readers, I think it is healthier to face the truth than to hide from it. I was depressed and angry at times while writing—angry because my country, which claims to be protecting democracy, human rights, and environmental quality, is doing the opposite both at home and abroad, all in an effort to maintain the American way of life. Although this sadness and anger remains, as I face the end of all we had valued I also feel a more intense appreciation of the beauty we can still enjoy. Beyond this, we can enjoy the challenge of creating a more fulfilling lifestyle after oil.

PART ONE

CHAPTER I

A NATION IN DENIAL ABOUT OIL

This book begins with an elucidation of the values that make it so difficult to break out of our national addiction to oil. Then, in Part Two, we examine the emerging spiritual values that could help us overcome the denial that accompanies our addiction. It builds on the work of those who provide evidence that oil production will soon peak Recently published books that discuss this evidence include *The Long Emergency* by James Howard Kunstler (2005) and *The Party's Over* and *Powerdown* by Richard Heinberg (2005 and 2004). The book by Julian Darley, *High Noon for Natural Gas*, (2004) covers a related subject. These writers rely on experts that include petroleum geologists such as M. K. Hubbert, Colin Campbell, Kenneth Deffeyes, L. F. Ivanhoe, and Walter Youngquist. These are sometimes called the "Cassandras" who give us the bad news. There are also the "cornucopians" such as Peter Huber, Michael C. Lynch, and Bjorn Lomborg who argue that resources are virtually infinite if the price is right. Richard Heinberg evaluates the conflicting claims of these two groups and sides with the Cassandras, partly because they are mostly geologists while the cornucopians are often economists whose optimism is based on faith in economic theory rather than on geological science. (1)

Books on this general topic continue to be published. Matthew R. Simmons published*Twilight in the Desert* in 2005. Simmons is an energy investment banker who has, for years, closely followed oil production data in Saudi Arabia and he argues that Saudi Arabia has long over-estimated or over-reported its reserves. This charge was reinforced by Colin Campbell who showed that most of the Arab countries reported a doubling of their reserves during the 1980s, mostly between 1987 and 1988. (2) Much of Simmons' data is based on a series of technical papers written by scientists, including some from Saudi Aramco, the

Saudi oil company, and published by the Society of Petroleum Engineers. These papers reveal problems that contradicted the optimistic forecast of virtually unlimited oil in Saudi Arabia. Simmons repeatedly complains that no one is planning how their country and the world can manage after oil production peaks and becomes much more expensive. But more expensive oil, he says can be a blessing not a curse. He emphasizes that "the world still works beyond Peak Oil," (3) or that it could continue to work with higher prices. He does think and write as a banker who assumes higher prices will stimulate new energy sources and that people can afford to pay them.

Early in 2006 another book was published by an energy analyst, Peter Tertzakian, who, though he was very reluctant to discuss the possibility of a peak in oil production, nonetheless did report that by 2005 "the overall average global decline rate is now somewhere between five and eight percent" (4) Notice that he is reporting an absolute decline and this at a time when demand for oil by China and India is beginning to increase, along with growing demand in the United States. Tertzakian goes on to point out that markets are very sensitive because of tight supplies and that hoarding is a threatening possibility which could cause a "breakpoint." After this prices would rise exponentially.

Most of the writers on peak oil argue that those who expect some technological breakthrough which will provide a substitute for oil are indulging in wishful thinking at this time. These possible substitutes either have horrendous environmental effects, or take more energy to produce than they provide, or require more capital than is available in our indebted society. Moreover, there may no longer be enough time to develop energy alternatives even if new ones are discovered and made available. The Hirsch Report, prepared for the U. S. Department of Energy in 2005, argues that a twenty-year lead time in the development of alternatives is needed before peak oil if fuel shortages are to be averted. (5) Thus there may have been a time when a relatively easy transition to renewable sources of energy sufficient to power a steady-state economic system was possible, but each passing year makes this transition more difficult. Americans have been so accustomed to having more and more that even a shift from continued economic growth to a steady state does not seem very likely to happen by choice. And, once the end of economic growth is forced upon us by the end of cheap oil, there may no longer be enough time or capital to make the transition to renewable sources of energy possible.

We in American society are so accustomed to having an ample supply of cheap oil that we may not be aware of what oil actually does for us. David and Marcia Pimentel have put this in perspective by explaining how much work a gallon of gasoline does. A gallon of gasoline, burned at 20% efficiency in an internal combustion engine does the equivalent of 6200 kcal of work, or work equal to 97 manpower hours. (6) If gasoline is $2.50 per gallon and labor is $10.00 per hour, fifteen minutes of human work buys a gallon of gasoline which can replace 97 manpower hours of work with a dollar value of $970. As a result we enjoy a high standard of living; oil does most of our physical work. In our society only 0.17% of the work done is done by human muscle. (7) As oil prices rise human labor will gradually regain its bargaining power, but not until oil is actually scarce, since it is so cheap relative to labor. Most likely the economic effects of high energy prices will be the driving force for change.

It should be self-evident that whether the peak in oil and gas production occurs in five years or in ten years or even in fifteen years, the suggestions put forth in this book are timely and valid. It takes a long time for cultural attitudes to change and for new policies to be put into practice. Changes in our external circumstances as the era of cheap oil draws to a close may open new religious possibilities and lead to new values. Once people realize that the age of cheap oil is over it is quite possible that a new religious orientation will be widely adopted. Books like this may help to point the way once people are ready to look for a way.

The working hypothesis that underlies this book is that peak oil is, or will soon be, curtailing the supply of oil in the world. The amount of oil in the ground is finite. But this does not mean that above-ground factors may also contribute to high prices and limited supply. There is a tendency for people to blame the oil companies for profiteering, or "speculators" for adding to the price of oil. And this may be true. The business community knows how to transform long-term shortages into short-term profit. But oil companies probably know, better than most of us, that the rare new discoveries of oil are offset by the general decline in the rate of extraction. The limits of so-called "tar sands" or "shale oil," which require enormous amounts of water as they are processed, are the scarcity of water.

Meanwhile, the vast majority of Americans remain in denial about the end of cheap oil and what it will do to change the American way of life. As some awareness of an impending energy crisis emerged through higher prices at the gasoline pumps, the political response was to turn to bio-fuels as a replacement for oil. Even the proponents of renewable energy jumped on this bandwagon. The American Solar Energy Society focused on "Breaking the Nation's Addiction to Oil" in its May-June, 2007 issue of *Solar Today*. The main emphasis was that business could continue as usual if we are clever about developing substitutes for oil. The articles were written by the good technophiles, evaluating renewable sources of energy, but they were still focused on maintaining the automobile society. There was virtually no recognition of what higher prices for the renewable substitutes would do to the poor in our society and very little recognition of the fact that bio-fuels might not be sustainable in an agricultural context. The fact that many Mexicans could no longer afford tortillas as prices for corn rose, due to increased demand for ethanol, was not mentioned, nor was the fact that U.S. exports of grain to needy people in Asia were curtailed as corn was diverted to ethanol production. Eventually, as natural gas is too expensive to provide nitrogen fertilizer and agricultural yields decline, land will be needed for food production. Our American love affair with the automobile is blinding us to the fact that it is sustainable only for the rich at the expense of the poor. We are in denial because we lack the moral and spiritual courage to look at the whole picture.

I am writing in the hope that this general outline of how our spiritual orientation needs to change may contribute, in the near term, to help people question the folly of making economic growth their main aim in life. The sooner we shift gears to a slower steady state the less suffering there will be if or when the crash comes. Reducing our dependence on oil will also reduce the pollution caused by burning oil, including emissions of carbon dioxide. In the long term, if there is a crash, it is my hope that this book will help people adjust to their new circumstances. It should be clear that if the nations of the world can avoid using nuclear weapons in the resource wars to come, and if the so-called greenhouse gases accumulating in the atmosphere do not render the planet uninhabitable, I am assuming that at least some people will survive the coming hard times in every part of the world. Because Americans still have more natural resources and land per capita, and fewer people, it is likely that most of us could survive. The real dangers we face in the years ahead are not physical but social, especially if people refuse to adapt and start blaming and fighting each other. The new spiritual orientation this book points to is intended primarily for American readers, partly because Americans have the most difficult spiritual transformation to make—from always having and expecting more—to being satisfied with much less. We certainly failed to make this transition thirty years ago.

The First Energy Crisis—The One we Forgot About

One of the ways we can estimate whether Americans are ready to recognize that the end of cheap oil is upon us is to compare the current energy crisis to the energy crisis of the 1970s.

Many of us remember the long lines at the gasoline pumps in the final months of 1973 after the oil embargo by OPEC (Organization of Petroleum Exporting Countries). This followed the fact that oil production in the United States peaked around 1970 as was predicted by M. K. Hubbert in 1956. After that this country lost its ability to control oil prices and the Arabs flexed their muscle for political ends and imposed an embargo on oil exports to the United States and eventually raised prices. (8)

The departure of the Shah from Iran in 1979, and his replacement by fundamentalist Muslims led by Ayatollah Khomeini, created the second act of the energy crisis of the Seventies. This came during the administration of Jimmy Carter who had already been exercising strong leadership in programs of energy conservation and providing subsidies for the development of renewable energy. There was a major cultural evolution from the counter-culture of the Sixties to energy conservation, appropriate technology and homesteading in the back-to-the-land movement of the Seventies. Some of this was precipitated by the energy crisis. Amory Lovins published an important book in 1977 called *Soft Energy Paths* which had the significant subtitle: *Toward a Durable Peace*. The prescient implication was that the hard paths (fossil fuels and nuclear power) were leading to resource wars. As a life-long pacifist with a Mennonite upbringing, I certainly resonated with these moral implications of energy conservation and renewable energy.

At this point, in the late Seventies, America had a chance to join the rest of the world in more moderate energy use. We all remember what happened, or should remember. As the decade of the Seventies ended Americans voted Ronald Reagan into office and he made it his priority to defeat the "evil empire" of the Soviets. He also junked the solar panels Carter had put on the White House roof and ended all the subsidies for the development of renewable energy. He was so vindictive that he even refused to read the "Global 2000" Report that had been prepared for him and cut funding for the agencies that had contributed to it. This ended the movement toward soft energy paths and led on a total reliance on fossil fuels. Because of Carter's emphasis on conservation and more intensive oil production there was a glut of oil and it was cheap. More subsidies and tax breaks were given to the oil corporations and as we moved on through the Nineties they made a lot of money as Americans bought gas-guzzling sports utility vehicles.

Andrew Bacevich has suggested that the energy crisis during the Carter administration marked the beginning of World War IV, the war over resources. He emphasized repeatedly that Reagan's victory over Carter revealed the will of the American people in a decisive manner. "The answer to whatever crisis afflicted the United States was to be found not in conservation or reduced expectations and surely not in spiritual renewal; it was to be found in the restoration of U. S. military might, which held the promise of enabling Americans always to have more rather than to make do with less." (9) Here we have one author's answer to the question which is driving our inquiry in this book: how can Americans, who have always had more . . . adapt to having less? So far we have to admit that Bacevich is correct: the majority of Americans follow Reagan in denial as they refuse to adapt to the end of oil. But, while the military solution (which is imposed on Americans and the rest of the world) will use a lot of oil, it does not produce oil and even if it grasps control of all the oil on the globe, it will eventually be gone. Also, the second reason for giving up fossil fuels, the fact that they cause global warming, is gaining support from many Americans.

Twenty years later we had a second chance to change our energy policy. We could have elected Al Gore, author of the environmental book, *Earth in the Balance*, and he might have promoted policies for conservation and the development of renewable energy. Instead, the American people, with a little help from the Supreme Court, elected George W. Bush. Both he and Vice President Cheney were oil men and there is evidence that they knew that the rate of oil extraction was likely to peak in this decade. They consulted with Matthew Simmons, mentioned above, a Republican energy investment banker who had consistently warned of an imminent oil peak—even in Saudi Arabia. (10)

Behind the scenes, meanwhile, geopolitical strategists like Zbigniew Brzezinski had been thinking about how the United States could maintain global dominance in the time of the end of oil. Michael Ruppert has written a long book which links the events of 9/11 with the end of oil.

Here is a lengthy quotation: "As Zbigniew Brzezinski had written in 1979, the 'immediate' task was to develop and simultaneously control a 'direct external threat' to manufacture an attack 'like a new Pearl Harbor,' that required a credible (at least in the public mind) and well-developed enemy. The need for this kind of attack was mentioned by the Project for a New American Century (PNAC) in its September 2000 report *Rebuilding American Defenses*. Such an attack would then provide a pretext for massive sequential military intervention to secure the energy supplies of the Middle East . . . . The essential thing would be that terrorists or their 'allies' must conveniently turn up in each needed area on schedule." (11) This document on *Rebuilding American Defenses* was prepared by the neo-conservatives in the Bush White House.

After the destruction of the World Trade Center towers on September 11, 2001, which may have been allowed to happen or even facilitated by the Bush administration, as some have argued, (12) there was a rationale for overt military action in the Middle East, first in Afghanistan and then in Iraq. After 9/11 the Administration was very adroit in using fear as the justification for, and driving force, in foreign policy. Although the U.S. had been establishing military bases in the Middle East and elsewhere all through the 1990s, (13) this process was intensified by the Bush Administration. The era of resource wars had begun. Misled by the pretext of fighting terrorism a large majority of Americans supported these military forays, at least for the first couple of years. By late 2005 and 2006 President Bush's popularity was already waning. The Iraqi insurgency not only killed many in the armed forces and many more Iraqis, it seemed successful in reducing the amount of Iraqi oil being exported. Some people, a growing number, are also aware of the irony of wasting precious energy resources in a war which was likely generated by the need for a secure supply of oil.

The Precocious Vision of the Seventies

As we begin living through our second energy crisis those who remember the first may be tempted to say "been there, done that." A considerable literature of gloom and doom emerged in the Seventies. Much of it predicted a coming era of scarcity, books with titles like *Muddling Toward Frugality* by Warren Johnson, *The End of Affluence* by Paul and Anne Ehrlich, *Ecology and the Politics of Scarcity* by William Ophuls, and *An Inquiry into the Human Prospect* by Robert Heilbroner. The fact that affluence instead of scarcity characterized the decade after the Seventies certainly helped to discredit the prophets of doom. On the other hand, authors like those cited may have been off only in their timing. In the books by Richard Heinberg and James Howard Kunstler we find very similar predictions of scarcity and hard times ahead.

The similarities between energy crisis books of the Seventies and the books of this decade are striking. Paul and Ann Ehrlich complained that the energy crisis "arrived during an administration unparalleled for its dishonesty and stupidity, one that even more than most was bought and paid for by industry," (14) referring to the Nixon administration. Richard Heinberg echoes these sentiments: "In the current Bush administration we see a combination of gross incompetence, high criminality, and almost limitless power—and this in the context of a time that requires the deftest and most visionary of leadership." (15) Or, to give one more example, The Ehrlichs gave us many pages of advice on the development of survival skills and self-reliant practices with special emphasis on raising food. Heinberg does the same (16) and this is good advice, both then and now. It made me realize that the School of Homesteading I conducted during the Seventies was not inappropriate. The idea of homesteading as an alternative to energy-intensive agriculture was promoted by a number of writers during the Seventies. Howard T. Odum concluded a paper on energy and human values with the proposal that churches should promote more homesteading opportunities. (17)

One of the significant effects of the energy crisis of the 1970s was the so-called migration reversal. For the first time in our national history a higher percentage of people moved from urban to rural areas than from rural to urban areas. This back-to-the-land movement coincided with the new homesteading movement and included many people who set out for the countryside seeking a self-reliant way of life, raising food for their families. It is certainly likely that a back-to-the-land movement can be expected again as the anxiety over peak oil becomes more widespread.

The vision of the Seventies may have been precocious, but the hard truth is that the warnings of scarcity in the Seventies are even more relevant now than they were then. But, because they came before people were ready to hear them, they were largely ignored. And they are ignored now because they are "old news". So it may seem as if the writings of the Seventies on this topic were wasted, along with social movements such as the homesteading movement of the back-to-the-land decade, the appropriate technology movement, and efforts in energy conservation. On the other hand, these things may be rediscovered in a time of expensive energy. The earlier warnings came when the rate of oil extraction in the United States peaked. As a result of energy conservation efforts under Carter, along with new discoveries prompted by the prospect of oil shortages, there was enough oil to carry us to the next crisis, which is likely to be upon us soon. Heinberg pointed out the important fact that a literal "peak" in global production would be visible only on a graph which showed oil production over at least 500 years. In a shorter time period the "peak" would more likely be seen as a plateau with a lot of ups and downs over a period of at least 40 years beyond 1973. The Association for the Study of Peak Oil has suggested that oil production might finally peak in 2007. *(18)* Or, as Peter Tertziakian suggested, above, the peak may have already occurred. The ups and downs on the plateau occur because of variations in demand and supply.

In any case, the heroic attempts to discover and extract more oil may eventually be seen as a really ambiguous achievement, partly because they distract policy-makers from the fact that burning oil is damaging to the climate. It may turn out that it would have been much better if we had shifted to steady state economics and renewable energy sources early in the years of the oil plateau. We can understand why this is so as we begin to understand the concept of carrying capacity. In the meantime, once oil production literally declines relative to the demand for it and a bidding war for it begins we will experience the shortage of oil in the form of prices we cannot afford to pay.

Carrying Capacity and Overshoot

The fact that global population was able to grow from around four billion in the mid-seventies to nearly six and a half billion in thirty years is a profoundly ambiguous achievement. Seen under the old paradigm, the economic paradigm, this is a great achievement since it presupposes the economic growth that gave nearly two and a half billion more people the privilege of life. Seen in the light of a new and still emerging paradigm, an ecological paradigm, this was a tragic achievement because it very likely exceeded the carrying capacity of the planet. Carrying capacity refers to the number of people the planet can support in a sustainable manner. Since human population grew very rapidly as the industrial revolution gained momentum, and since this growth was made possible by fossil fuels, which are nonrenewable and will soon be increasingly expensive and eventually unavailable, it may become impossible to provide adequate food for the population that oil made possible. Because food has been cheap and abundant, at least in the United States, many people are unaware of the energy used in food production. The Pimentels, again, provide numbers to understand this. In Mexico about 1144 hours of manpower is needed to produce one hectare of corn; in the United States only 12 hours of man power is expended to produce a hectare of corn, with oil making up the difference. (19) Oil is needed for mechanized modes of production on the farm, for the mining and manufacture of fertilizer and farm equipment, for food processing, for transportation in our global supermarket, and for the manufacture of pesticides. Natural gas, another main fossil fuel, is used to make nitrogen fertilizer which has increased the yields of crops to keep pace with increased population. Supplies of gas have been limited for a variety of reason, one of which is that it is much harder to transport than oil.

Although "carrying capacity," as an ecological term, has long been used in scientific ecological literature to describe the limiting factors in animal populations, William R. Catton, Jr., was one of the first to apply this term to human population on a global level. His book, *Overshoot*, published in 1980, is such an urgent plea for understanding this human dilemma that it is a truly alarming book. He begins by explaining that humankind is locked into a system that can provide life only by stealing from the future. We are in diachronic competition with our descendents. He goes on to explain that "a major aim of this book is to show that commonly proposed 'solutions' for problems confronting mankind are actually going to aggravate those problem s." (20) We can see how this is illustrated in the paragraph above: using oil to provide food for a growing population until the oil is no longer affordable deprives the next generation of oil and food and life.

Throughout history humans have devised ways of enlarging the carrying capacity of their environment. Catton describes the basic strategies used to do this. Two such strategies are takeover and drawdown. As agriculture emerged some ten thousand years ago, people took over wild areas and used them to raise domesticated crops and livestock. The invention of weapons, especially guns, enabled the takeover of wild animals for food or their habitat for more land. As Europe became overpopulated in the sixteenth and seventeenth centuries the land of North and South America was taken over by settlers who considered the land empty and unsettled. Diseases and genocidal practices they brought with them did indeed soon make the land empty and open for takeover. As the wonderful land that soon became known as the United States was settled its superabundant resources gave settlers a feeling that these resources were limitless. The Culture of Exuberance was born and it contributes enormously to the ethos of expansiveness that needs to be overcome if humans are to survive.

Around 1800, when there was not much left to take over, carrying capacity was enlarged by another strategy known as drawdown. Existing resources were used more intensively, and soon the use of fossil fuels was instrumental in making this possible. Food production was augmented by drawing on "fossil acreage". This included the pumping of water from very slowly recharged aquifers for irrigation which then literally suffered "drawdown". As Catton pointed out repeatedly, the success of such drawdown strategies was always temporary because they degraded the ecological basis of natural productivity. In other words, they did not result in a sustainable increase in carrying capacity. Each of these methods was also accompanied by its particular forms of pollution, just as burning fossil fuels added gases to the atmosphere which create acid rain or the greenhouse effect and the virtual certainty of damaging climate change.

Among the inventions that have contributed to the number of humans on the globe, perhaps the most important was the Haber-Bosch process for the production on nitrogen fertilizer. Two recent books on food and agriculture are focused on corn, a cheap-food crop that is over-produced and therefore underpriced. Both of these books argue the folly of such over-production from the grower's point of view as it lowers prices, and both list its negative impact on human health and on the environment. Most importantly, both make it clear that this enormous crop of corn is made possible by the ammonium nitrate which is made by the Haber-Bosch process. Farmers are no longer limited by being dependent on manure or other organic sources of nitrogen fertilizer; they now have synthetic nitrogen fertilizer made out of fossil fuels, mostly natural gas. Michael Pollan quotes geographer Vaclav Smil who calculated that two out of every five people alive today would not have been alive without Haber's invention. (21) According to journalist George Pyle, without synthetic nitrogen, Earth's current population of six billion people would be no more than 4 billion." (22) This may be some indication of what sort of die-off might be expected in the next century when the oil and gas is gone—if the human population is not reduced in other ways. Another book, by a very young man, argues that global population will be reduced to around 500 million during the next 50 to 100 years. (23) His book generally presents a truly apocalyptic picture of the end of cheap oil, although he apparently failed to notice that food has been and can be raised without oil. But he is right to warn that a die-off is possible and likely.

Catton's book may be offensive to many readers, partly because he makes the ambiguities in the human rise to civilization so clear. But a larger part of the problem with his book is that he writes as an angry sociologist, and the book communicates that anger. What Catton is writing about is the tragic dilemma of humanity, and, since it is not caused by simple stupidity, it should not engender anger. Fritz Haber received the Nobel Prize in 1920 for "improving the standards of agriculture and the well-being of mankind." (24) His achievement, like so many others, is tragic because humans act in heroic ways to improve their well-being with the best of intentions. But, given the paradigm under which they function, their heroic efforts only make the problems worse. Were this story told by a writer with a tragic sense of life, we would feel pity and terror as we witness these ill-fated human achievements, and, after the arousal and purgation of these emotions, as Aristotle explained, we would have found peace and a deeper understanding, but not the anger and revulsion that Catton's book communicates.

Every great technological achievement has its negative consequences as well. The Haber-Bosch process that gave us synthetic nitrogen fertilizer also provided for the manufacture of explosives that made the Nazi war effort possible. More recently ammonium nitrate has served as a key ingredient in the manufacture of methamphetamines resulting in "meth" as a cheap but very destructive drug.

Perhaps the most ambiguous of these achievements is the one that began in mid-nineteenth century with improvements in public health, vaccinations, and antibiotics. These methods of death control emerged too rapidly to be offset by methods of birth control and populations exploded. Again, who can speak against this from within the old paradigm? In fact it is only from the newer ecological paradigm that we are able to recognize that all this marvelous technology has very likely led the human population to overshoot the carrying capacity of the earth. Even from this perspective many of us would probably want to save lives now in hopes that somehow there will be enough resources for those who come after us. In less complex animal populations an overshoot leads to a crash, or die-off. Can humans somehow circumvent this conclusion without relying on further damaging drawdown strategies? This book suggests that a basic change in our technologies, and acceptance of a steady state in economics reinforced by a compatible spiritual orientation, may at least mitigate human suffering and loss.

The Long Overdue Need for Limits to Growth

In 1972 the first version of *The Limits to Growth* was published. In it the authors, Donella H. Meadows, Dennis L. Meadows, and Jorgen Randers, urged that the rate of economic and population growth must be reduced to a level commensurate with resource availability. They pointed out that if population and economic growth were allowed to continue growth at exponential rates the result would be an overshoot of carrying capacity and the possibility of crash within one hundred years.

The Meadows book was sponsored by the Club of Rome, a small international group of concerned people which included industrial and governmental leaders. In 1974 a second report to the Club of Rome was published, *Mankind at the Turning Point*, by Mihaijlo Mesarovic and Eduard Pestel, which, instead of modeling the world as one highly aggregated world system, divided the world into ten regions. It also called for differentiation in kinds of growth to redress the inequities that exist between different regions of the earth. It emphasized, in the most urgent manner, that the rich nations must help the poorer nations in order to prevent mass starvation.

This emphasis was totally ignored by the rich countries, such as the United States. Another significant study published at this time was *The Global 2000*

Report to the President of the U. S. by Gerald Barney, the book that was ignored by President Reagan.

It was not surprising that these books, as they challenged the reigning orthodoxy of economic growth in such a direct and forceful manner, found widespread opposition. Two types of criticism were emphatic: that the authors did not consider exponential growth of technological capabilities as much as they considered growth of limiting factors, and that they were insensitive to ethical issues. To a large degree, however, the authors did express their awareness of these criticisms, especially in regard to technological possibilities. The ethical issue had to do with the problem of how to balance the needs of the present against the needs of the future. This issue was discussed above with reference to the tragic choices people have made when they maintain life in the present by stealing from posterity. (25)

In 1992 the authors of the first "Limits" book published a sequel called *Beyond the Limits*. The authors, recognizing that exponential growth has continued unchecked, acknowledge that human society has overshot its limits. They hold out the hope and show the possibility that a crash can be avoided if timely action is taken to make a correction or turnaround especially in the use of resources and in the generation of pollution. They postulated the possibility of a "sustainability revolution" on a magnitude comparable to the agricultural or industrial revolutions. And they were sanguine about renewable energy: "there is no scarcity of energy on earth. If the most sustainable, least polluting sources are used with high efficiency, it should be not only possible but affordable to power the needs of the human race sustainably" (26) This certainly was a possibility, but, despite some relatively small scale wind farms, it did not happen by 2005. A world of nation states, in competition with each other, and without strong international leadership, can hardly be expected to act in the common interest of mankind.

On the other hand, *Beyond the Limits* does point to some successes. There is the example of the Montreal Protocol, the international agreement to phase out chlorofluorocarbons (CFCs) in the upper atmosphere which destroy the ozone that provides protection from ultra-violet rays. Although it is a slow process, the nations of the world acting through the United Nations, did take action to protect the earth. This example, however, must be balanced by the more recent fact that the United States, which produces the lion's share of carbon dioxide, refused to sign on to the Kyoto Agreement to limit that greenhouse gas, even though nearly all other countries did sign.

Finally, in 2005 the authors of the limits books published another sequel, *Limits to Growth: The 30-Year Update*. Although the authors clearly emphasize that the ecological footprint of humanity has overgrown what the earth can continue to support, so that we are in the overshoot mode, they remain moderately optimistic that humanity can avoid the collapse of its global ecosystems. The two major problems are to reduce the resources we now consume and to reduce the pollution now generated so that the ecological sinks are not eroded or "filled". This requires the kinds of changes that are listed in chapter III below, and it is a big order. At this point we are in the overshoot and oscillation mode in which growth alternates above and below carrying capacity. This is an extremely risky period of time.

I see two problems in this third update of the "limits" books. First, it does not include enough data on the possibility of economic constraints, or even collapse, as that which might make the transition to sustainability difficult or impossible Second, although the authors do include carbon dioxide among the pollutants that stretch the capacity of ecological sinks of pollution, (27) they do not very forcefully emphasize it as the most likely cause of ecological collapse. In early 2008 we are bombarded with data about the melting of the glaciers in Greenland and in the polar regions. The positive feedback loops of more storms killing more trees, melting tundra releasing more methane, a much more potent greenhouse gas, and other disasters waiting to happen, may very likely make climate change inevitable and rapid. Even more discouraging data is provided by Lester R. Brown in his recent book, *Outgrowing the Earth: The Food Security Challenge in An Age of Falling Water Tables and Rising Temperatures*. All this makes the reduction in fossil fuel use more urgent than the authors of *Limits to Growth* express when they say that oil will still be available and natural gas will last for a longer period of time.

Social and Economic Effects of a Global Oil Peak

The literature we have reviewed so far in this chapter reflects a wide range of opinion on how severe the effects of the global oil peak will be. To begin with, a peak means that only half of the oil in the ground has been used, while the other half remains to be extracted. Unfortunately, this is the half that is harder to find and harder to get. Most of it is in politically-hostile territory. Obviously when more energy is required to get that oil than is in the oil, it may be left in the ground. Nonetheless, there will be oil for many years, but because the demand for it exceeds the supply, it will be more expensive, and it is the cost of oil that will affect human societies. The energy investment banker, Matthew Simmons, has no doubt that prices will rise, and beyond suggesting that $200 per barrel may be still be too low, he does not speculate on how high the price might go. (28) Michael Ruppert reported that in conversation with him Matthew Simmons predicted that when oil sells for $182 per barrel, gasoline at the pump will be about $7.00 per gallon. (29) If the price of gasoline went up to ten dollars per gallon it would make life difficult for many people in the United States but it is likely that we could adapt with the development of more mass transit and the reopening of more railroad tracks and inter-urban light rail. This, of course, also requires some political initiative.

But what about food production, often cited as the most energy-intensive industry? Both

James Howard Kunstler and Richard Heinberg offer very pessimistic outlooks on food. Certainly the industrial mode of food production is not sustainable, and it will change. But it is the easiest thing to change. According to Barbara Kingsolver, at least one fourth of the households in America already raise some of their food in backyard or community gardens. (30) According to surveys that were sponsored by the National Gardening Association, nearly half of the households in America raised some vegetables. This was true during the Seventies, the back-to-the-land decade, but backyard gardening has a long history and a fully developed infrastructure with many sources of the seeds and tools that are needed. And it continues to thrive even without economic necessity or government support. People who are not in a position to produce their own food may find that rapidly rising prices will provide an incentive to move to where they can do so, or find sources of food grown close to where they live by growers using organic and energy-conserving methods.

Industrial agriculture as it is now practiced will certainly have to change and, with more expensive sources of chemical fertilizers and pesticides, some producers will survive only as they change to organic methods which even now use 30% less oil. This also requires changes in the structure of agriculture. As animal manure replaces chemical fertilizers, farms will once again need to be more diversified with a mixture of crops and livestock, especially after natural gas shortages makes ammonium nitrate fertilizer too costly. The specialized agribusiness operations will need to be replaced by small-scale farms as we become a neo-agrarian society. We can hope that the function of the market will facilitate many of these changes. But it can also give false signals, for example, if people want to continue driving their cars and demand more biofuels to do so. If more land is diverted to raising crops for fuels while food production might be curtailed by lack of nitrogen fertilizer or very expensive pesticides, there could be food shortages and higher prices. This, in turn, would pressure more people to raise food for themselves, assuming that land will be available. I think we can be sanguine about the prospect of enough affordable food in this country. This assumes that the inflation generated by rising energy prices can be accommodated without causing economic upheaval. And it assumes that climate changes will hold off long enough to allow for the transition to an agrarian society. Most importantly, it assumes that people will actually be willing to give up their dependence on the global supermarket. That which is physically necessary, must also be politically and socially acceptable.

People who depend on gas and oil for home heating may be able to invest in better insulation and more efficient energy use. People who heat with gas certainly should have time to do this, especially if the oil peak precedes the gas peak and if people take the first peak as a warning. But a caveat is in order here. It has generally been assumed that natural gas will peak later than oil, in about 2020. (31) But Julian Darley argued, more recently, that in the United States oil and gas may peak at the same time, especially as gas rapidly replaces oil. (32)

It is tempting to suggest that Americans in this richest of rich countries have enough discretionary money to easily manage higher prices. But this may no longer be the case for several reasons. First, the current generation of Americans, who seek instant gratification with credit cards, is not accustomed to saving money. Many have large credit card debt loads. Second, on a national level, the Bush policy of trying to secure supplies of oil through military means has been extremely costly. We now have a national debt estimated at around nine trillion dollars. The generation that will have to pay this debt is the generation that will need more capital to make the transition to a renewable energy economy. And the people who will be paying higher energy bills will be taxed more heavily as well. The third problem is that because of the net transfer of wealth from the poor to the rich, especially during this administration with its tax cuts for the rich, the people who will need more money to pay higher energy costs no longer have it. There is no doubt that many people even in this country will be totally impoverished as the cost of oil rises. Hopefully, the administration that replaces the Bush-Cheney regime will be less ideological and more truly compassionate.

Another problem lies in the fact that the United States has become a debtor nation and as a result there is the very real possibility that the euro could replace the dollar as the world's major currency in the sale of oil. Various nations, with a variety of motivations, have been proposing that the euro, being stronger than the dollar, should replace the dollar. William R. Clark has pointed out that it was after Saddam Hussein decided to sell oil for euros rather than dollars that Iraq was invaded. (33) If Iran gets its oil bourse going, or if OPEC decides to sell oil in euros rather than dollars, the United States would suffer serious economic losses. Or it might begin bombing Iran, as it seems tempted to do.

Although a complete transition to an energy economy based on renewables may take many years, assuming there will be capital available for its development instead of being squandered in resource wars, it is quite reasonable to postulate a transitional phase of about ten years after the oil has peaked and begins to cost much more. During these years there will continue to be supplies of oil and gas for those who can afford them. Coal, although the most polluting fuel, is abundant. If this transition is accepted by a sizable majority of the people, along with a new set of values and a new ecological paradigm, it could be a transition to a steady-state agrarian society. But if a substantial number of people remain addicted to the old economic paradigm, and are willing to fight to get more at the expense of others, the transition may lead only to the kind of social disintegration envisioned by writers like James Howard Kunstler. He sees only a few parts of the country (which would be without central government and fragmented into semi-autonomous regions) able to survive with a modicum of social order.

I cannot leave this topic without mentioning a book that is of great value in clarifying the issues we have raised in this section: *Ecology and the Politics of Scarcity Revisited*. It was written by William Ophuls and first published in 1977. When I read it then I thought it was unduly harsh in its political solutions. Now, as I read the version revised by A. Stephen Boyan, the "Revisited" version, I was ready for it and recognized its value. The book recognizes that "growth is the secular religion of American society, providing a social goal, a basis for political solidarity, and a source of individual motivation" He also points out that, "all societies display social fanaticism to some extent. Their first response to threatening doubts is to redouble their efforts to shore up belief in the current paradigm, which is after all a kind of civil religion." (34) As long as the destructive economic paradigm is prevalent in society, Ophuls recommends Garret Hardin's solution of "mutual coercion, mutually agreed upon by the majority of the people affected." (35) But Ophuls recognizes that a police state is not a long term answer and concludes, in the final chapter, with the expectation of a change of heart, a metanoia, as Americans willingly accept the ecological paradigm and recognize that a steady-state agrarian economy is the only sustainable way. In chapter III below I will try to list the kinds of changes needed to bring this about. And in Part Two of this book we will explore the possibility of a new spiritual orientation.

When Catton opened his book with reference to how we are locked into a system that forces us to steal from the future, we who read it now, twenty five years later, have to recognize that we are likely the first generation of that future. And even we have not yet ceased to steal from those who come after us, or from the poorer and more powerless people of the world with the exploitive economic policies of the United States. This may be because we already have less than those of the previous generation. In the next chapter I will try to trace this selfishness in the American way of life to those values that have deep roots in our history and cultural tradition.

CHAPTER II

CULTURAL ROOTS OF OUR DENIAL OF LIMITS

Stewart Udall, who had been Secretary of the Interior under President Carter, wrote a "Foreward" to Catton's *Overshoot* in which he reflected on how the energy crisis of the Seventies chastened the optimism of the decades that preceded. He recognized that a basic change in orientation was necessary. "To accept the hard part of belt-tightening and sacrifices, we must first trim back our technological optimism. We need, in short, something we lost in our haste to remake the world: a sense of limits, an awareness of the importance of earth's resources." (1) It is not easy for us, in this more troubled time in history, to remember that a mere fifty years ago the American people and their leaders believed there were no limits to material resources, energy. or technological ingenuity. Above all, they believed in progress—and some still do!

The Culture of Exuberance in America

As we reviewed the response of at least some people to the interruptions in oil supplies during the Seventies in the previous chapter it was plain to see that technological optimism was no longer universal. At the same time we recognized the fact that when energy supplies were restored in the Eighties, people, aided by the advertising of those who profit from economic growth, promptly forgot that oil was a finite resource. In their exuberance Americans bought sports utility vehicles and burned gasoline as though it would be inexhaustible. We need to understand that the attitudes that underlie our culture of exuberance have deep roots in our history. In this chapter we shall try to uncover these roots, examine them, and evaluate them. They support a pernicious weed in our cultural landscape: the expectation and desire to have more at a time when there will be less.

When Europeans settled in America they came from overpopulated and often impoverished places. In contrast, this seemed like the Promised Land. During the latter half of the Twentieth Century, during the lifetime of most of us, we have lived in the richest country in the world. How this has shaped the American character is the subject of a book, *People of Plenty*, by David M. Potter. We now live in a country where shopping malls are our temples. Advertisers write our sacred scriptures. From the beginning, the vastness and richness of this land, along with the expectation by the settlers of making a new start, combined to create the expectation of paradise on earth. As Mircea Eliade explained in his essay on the mythical geography of paradise and utopia, the discovery and exploration of America was heavily freighted with the imagery of paradise—a New Beginning in a New World. (2) R.W.B. Lewis reviewed literary expressions of this idea in his book *The American Adam*. Cultural historians such as Charles L. Sanford, in *The Quest for Paradise*, and George H. Williams in *Wilderness and Paradise in Christian Thought*, among others, have evaluated the importance of this theme in American history. Eliade did recognize that the religious origins of these paradisiacal expectations were radically secularized, giving way to the myth of progress and the cult of youth and novelty. And, as we shall see, the attempt to recover the perfection of paradise found subsequent expression in diverse ways, such as the retreat to suburbia, on the popular level, and the development of technology, on the more sophisticated level.

Sacred History as a Religious Form

The expectation of always having more implies a linear conception of time and this, in turn, leads to the possibility of progress in time. Progress means moving forward. This idea is not universal; it has its roots in the Judeo-Christian tradition. The ancient Hebrews attributed their origin to the revelation of God at a moment in their history when He appeared to Moses and commanded him to lead his people out of slavery in Egypt. This theophany in history was a radically new religious form. Most theophanies, or revelations of the sacred beings, had been through natural phenomena prior to this. In his book, *Cosmos and History*, Mircea Eliade emphasizes the uniqueness of this new religious form in the context of those cosmic (natural or supernatural) religious forms that are found throughout the history of religions. Virtually all these embody a conception of cyclical time in which time, and the world, is annually abolished and then regenerated in New Year's festivals. The potential relevance and value of such structures of time in a post-petroleum future will be discussed in another chapter. Here we point out only that, according to Karl Lowith, "within a cyclic Weltanschauung and order of the universe, where every movement of advance is, at the same time, a movement of return, there is no place for progress." (3)

Sacred history, as a linear process, is a meaningful sequence from a Beginning, when the Hebrews escaped from Egypt, to an End, when the Messiah is expected. The time between beginning and end, Eliade explained, is also significant. "Directly ordered by the will of Yahweh, [the Hebrew name for God] history appears as a series of theophanies, negative or positive, each of which has intrinsic value." (4) And, just as God makes history by exercising his will, so humans also learned to make history through the exercise of will. In this respect man was made in the image of God and shares God's transcendence over nature.

As Lynn White pointed out in his influential essay, "The Historical Roots of our Ecologic Crisis," the creation myth in Genesis encouraged the development of an aggressive anthropocentric attitude. Humans were created after the earth had been created for them and were given lordship or dominion over the creation, along with the responsibility to care for it. Later, as Christianity spread over Europe, Lynn White argued that "the victory of Christianity over paganism was the greatest psychic revolution in the history of our culture . . . . By destroying pagan animism Christianity made it possible to exploit nature in a mood of indifference to the feelings of natural objects." (5) Certainly Christianity has seldom taught us to respect our fellow creatures. Moreover, as eco-feminists have charged, since men were taught to consider women as more natural than themselves, they, too, were exploited. (6)

Even though modern culture may be Post-Christian in many ways, our faith in perpetual progress is rooted in Judeo-Christian teleology, according to White. Although White may have failed to recognize that Christianity includes a complex mixture of other influences within it to account for some of the attitudes it seems to support, (as I argued in "Faustian Striving and the Gnostic Dimension in Western Civilization"), his charges against Christianity have much justification. White proposed St. Francis as a patron saint for ecologists because the early Franciscans recognized the spiritual autonomy of all parts of nature. We shall return to this spiritual emphasis in the second part of this book

As the heirs of ancient Judaism, Christians carried on this conception of sacred history, making Christ the center of history, as they divided time into BC and AD. Most Christians also continued to see history as a religious form, as the history of salvation. This is an important detail in our story because it opens the possibility of understanding even secular history as a process of continuing fulfillment toward the Kingdom of God. A qualification is in order here, however. Many scholars explain that eventually, over the centuries, the history of salvation was "individualized," "related to the salvation of each single soul." (7) This individualizing of sin and salvation became much more pronounced under the influence of capitalism as it promoted a selfish consumerism. While some

Christians may give lip service to the idea that they are part of the community of faith, this idea has found no deep expression in American life. According to Robert Bellah and his colleagues, "individualism lies at the very core of American culture." (8) As we shall see in subsequent chapters, the recovery of community will be absolutely essential after the time of cheap oil.

The individualised understanding of sin and salvation had the effect of preventing the social gospel proposed by religious thinkers such as Walter Rauschenbusch from taking root. Also, the notion of sacred history was difficult to maintain alongside the modern understanding of history as a secular phenomenon. Thus the notion of salvation history fell apart—into secular history on the one hand and a mythical conception of personal salvation, on the other. It is mythical rather than historical when salvation is understood in terms of the substitutionary theory of the atonement—that we are "saved" from an eternity in Hell by some arrangement made by divine beings to the effect that Christ's death on the cross offers salvation—if we believe in Him.

What remained, at least until the Nineteenth Century, was a sense of divine providence, the idea that God was in charge of, and active in, historical events. This did allow for a feeling of confidence and trust in the historical process. Then, as Lowith put it, thinkers like Comte "rejected divine providence categorically, replacing it by a belief in progress." (9) And, as we shall see, the ideology of progress takes many forms. One of the most significant was the belief in human perfectibility through human effort.

Religious Origins of Technological Progress

The Scientific Revolution of the Sixteenth century grew out of a Renaissance world in which magic and alchemy, Hermetic and Neoplatonic speculation, and other occult traditions were influential. In his review of the origins of science Lewis Mumford emphasizes the role of magic because it liberated proto-scientists to attempt the manipulation of nature. (10) Francis Bacon is often considered one of the first to move out of this welter of Renaissance magic and speculation and into actual observation and experiment. Bacon emphasized the aphorism "knowledge is power" and conceived of science as an organized and collective inquiry for the benefit of humanity. In this he differed from the many practitioners of magic at the time who usually worked secretly and alone and for private profit. The current distinction between pure and applied science may not have been recognized by Bacon, who sought knowledge about nature in order to control nature. As Carolyn Merchant summarized it, Bacon worked out of religious motivations as he sought to regain the dominion over nature which was lost in the Fall. "Before the Fall, there was no need for power or dominion, because Adam and Eve had been sovereign over all other creatures . . . . Only by 'digging further and further into the main of natural knowledge' could mankind recover that lost dominion." (11) Although this is an all-to-brief thumbnail sketch of the origin of science and technology, it does give substance to the idea of progress—recovery of the perfection that was our birthright before the Fall. And its cultural residue was our unquenchable technological optimism.

In his comprehensive discussion of the religious motivations behind the origin of science and technology, David Noble adds the millenarian emphasis, the idea that a new era was dawning. "Perhaps more than anyone else before or since, Bacon defined the Western project of modern technology, and his bold vision was 'framed with reference to the millennial expectation of man's dominion over nature.' For Bacon the sustained development of the useful arts offered the greatest evidence, and the best means, of millenarian advance." (12) Noble's entire book traces these religious motivations in many scientists throughout the history of Western science and technology, on to the exploration of space and finally to that questionable power that tempts technologists to create perfection through genetic engineering. We must not fail to notice, however, that the perfection or redemption of nature in this program requires the transmutation of the biosphere into a technosphere. This is a dominant version of technological progress. During the Industrial Revolution it was eventually mechanized, as it were, and measured by growth in the gross domestic product.

The conquest of nature with technology was thus present at the beginning of science and remained a powerful motivation of science and technology until the middle of the Twentieth century. The emergence of ecological awareness gradually called this project into question. If the American people had a chance to vote most would probably choose the ecological paradigm over the economic paradigm. But the corporations that rule the world and seem to control the current administration exert a powerful influence through media and advertising to remind the American people that they cannot afford to abandon the economic paradigm. Another paradigm is certainly possible. Although the Scientific Revolution was based on a mechanistic model of reality, it replaced an earlier organic model of reality, a process clearly described by Carolyn Merchant in *The Death of Nature*. In the concluding section of this book we shall see that an ecological model of reality, based on a view of the world as an organism, is emerging in our society. David Korten, as he tried to understand the dynamics of corporate acquisitiveness, found the metaphor of organism enlightening and ambiguous. Corporate growth is, in the economic world, comparable to cancer in an organism. Both grow at the expense of the host body until the body dies. Korten is explicit about this. "As I noted in the Prologue, cancer is more than a metaphor for the relationship of capitalism and the global corporation to the market and democracy. It is a clinical diagnosis. Think of capitalism as a defective genetic coding in our economic system that causes individual enterprises to seek their own unlimited growth without regard to the consequences for society." (13) In fact, corporate growth threatens not only society but the earth as a self-regulating organism.

Faust as Our Cultural Hero

We have been uncovering the roots of the American culture of exuberance, and at least two more roots remain to be uncovered: What is the meaning of the Faustian willingness to sell body and soul to the devil for knowledge and power, and how does the accumulation of money and power fit into all this?

The Faustian theme was first given literary expression by Christopher Marlowe, an Elizabethan dramatist who was a slightly older contemporary of Shakespeare. The Faust legend developed during the sixteenth century and it reflected the concerns of both the Protestant Reformation and the Renaissance. According to the legend Faust studied theology at the University of Wiittenburg in Germany and received his doctorate in Divinity. Marlowe clearly shows how the religious anxiety over salvation motivated Faust to renounce God and Christ. Faust knew the Lutheran teaching on the infinite distance separating man from God, and he knew that only faith could save him. But as a learned man, proud of his knowledge, he rejects the way of faith and turns to magic instead. Hoping to save himself he needs power over nature, and given the status of technology at the time, magic was his means of achieving it. The good angel in Faust's conscience warns Faust about such a blasphemy. but the bad angel urges him on to magic:

> Go forward, Faustus, in that famous art
> Wherein all nature's treasury is contained.
> Be thou on earth as Jove is in the sky,
> Lord and commander of these elements (I, 1, 75-79).

Notice how the bad angel appeals to Faust's desire for God-like power to exploit the treasures of nature. That night Faust learns how to conjure up demonic spirits, and as Mephistophiles rises to do his will Faust signs over body and soul to the devil provided he can be "a spirit in form and substance" (Act II, Scene 2, 95) for a period of 24 years. We can understand "spirit" in this context as the absolute will, unfettered by the physical and emotional constraints of body and soul.

In his *Tragical History of Doctor Faustus*, then, Marlowe is dramatizing the conflicts and tensions created by the promises of the Renaissance and the religious anxiety of the Protestant Reformation as they pressured seventeenth century man toward a new quest for knowledge and power. In his characterization of Faust as a demonic spirit, he portrayed the prototype of technological man; and in Faust's damnation, he expressed his estimate of the cost which this new and desperate adventure entailed. Faust is our cultural hero, just as Prometheus was for the ancient Greeks. He embodied what were to become our dominant cultural traits: our ceaseless search for knowledge and power to control nature, as well as the courage to risk damnation for it. Rene Dubos complained that "it is a distressing fact that the Faustus legend is the only important one created by Western civilization. The activities of the learned and dynamic Dr. Faustus symbolize our own restlessness and our eagerness to achieve mastery over men and the external world, irrespective of long-range consequences." (14)

Marlowe's Faust is almost a tragic hero, or he would have been heroic in his quest for knowledge and power except for the fact that this quest is metaphorically associated with the image of gluttony throughout the play. And just as gluttony or overeating is often the result of anxiety, so Faust is pathetic or less than tragic in that he is driven to seek knowledge and power because of his religious despair and anxiety. The bravado with which he risks damnation for the sake of knowledge at the outset erodes as the play progresses. This is most obvious in the middle part of the play as Faust, now able to do whatever he pleases, uses his power in trivial ways for petty personal satisfactions. He flatters an emperor with his necromantic display, delights a pregnant duchess with grapes out of season, insults the pope, and becomes increasingly vicious as he takes revenge on those who question his demonic powers. Marlowe portrayed Faust as one who became less than human as he tried to transcend the human condition. His character coarsens as the play progresses, an ironic development for one who gave up body and soul to be a spirit. Having cut himself off from humanity, he finds nothing worthwhile to do with his superhuman powers. Marlowe judged his protagonist severely, showing clearly how knowledge and power and wealth did not bring him happiness or human decency. As the scarcity of resources like oil begins to affect our well-being, Faustian striving will be even more dysfunctional as it becomes more frantic.

The Faust legend very explicitly introduces a demonic dimension into Western civilization; it diminishes the possibility of contentment or satisfaction. It is precisely such restless striving that is celebrated in Goethe's version of the Faust legend, and Goethe, early in the nineteenth century, most fully articulated the nature of Faust as our culture hero. At the end of Goethe's play his Faust is still seeking mastery over the physical world, supervising the draining of swamps (wetlands?) in order to develop more land for people. Goethe's Faust uses his demonic powers to accomplish vast utopian schemes which clearly anticipate the morally ambivalent technological triumphs of today. And he is saved at the end. As his soul ascends to heaven the angels sing:

> Should a man strive with all his heart,
> Heaven can foil the devil. (Part Two, V, 818-819)

Thus constant, restless striving, a life bereft of the present and thrust into the future, defines the human condition. The term "Faustian bargain" has also been used frequently by environmental writers to describe policies or strategies that provide short-term benefits at the risk of long term problems, particularly in the case of nuclear power, where the wastes are with us for thousands of years.

Is the term 'demonic' obsolete?

I have to insist that the term "demonic" has currency. The term "demonic" refers to a universal religious form, part of the dialectic of the divine and the demonic. The experience of the holy, or the sacred, is often ambivalent. Although most Western readers will understand demonic as a term in the religious terminology of Western religions, this is because most Western readers are familiar with the Judeo-Christian tradition. They thus know the demonic as the devil, or Satan, as a mythic projection of the demonic in the form of a supernatural person. But the demonic recurs as a religious form in every religious tradition and also in our so-called secular world. Any experience of super-human power that stands over and against a human being shows attributes of the demonic, especially when the power is totally devoid of compassion or human feeling. It must be added that this super-human power can also be seen as a force for the well-being of human beings in some way; this is the ambivalence of the divine-demonic phenomenon: Faust is our cultural hero.

Demonic Powers and Money

One way for us to get a handle on the issues we have been discussing here is to ask how much would be enough, for personal income, corporate growth, or gross domestic product, GDP. One exceptionally humane economist who did this was E. F. Schumacher, author of *Small is Beautiful: Economics as if People Mattered*. As a leading proponent of intermediate or appropriate technology, he was very critical of industrial technology. In an essay called "Technology with a Human Face," he points out that industrial "technology has no self-limiting principle—in terms, for instance, of size, speed, or violence." Later in this essay Schumacher goes on to argue that "any activity which fails to recognize a self-limiting principle is of the devil." (15)

Schumacher associated the demonic with the denial of limits and the restless striving that has been so characteristic of the culture of exuberance in industrial societies. In these societies it is the economy of the market system that most forcefully promotes more growth and most vehemently denies limits. Scott Burns, in a little book on the household economy, distinguishes it from the market economy. "The uniqueness of the market economy lies in its having no natural boundaries, no biological or natural constraints. It is a Faustian instrument, divorced from nature, with no inherent capacity for recognizing self-limiting factors." (16)

Many years ago the Greek philosopher Aristotle had recognized the difference between "oikonomia," which meant household management and is the origin of our word "economic," and "chrematistics," which referred to making money. Herman Daly and John Cobb comment on this distinction. "Unlimited accumulation is the goal of the chrematist and is evidence for Aristotle of the unnaturalness of the activity. True wealth is limited by the satisfaction of the concrete need for which it was designed. For oikonomia, there was such a thing as enough. For chrematistics, more is always better." (17) True Christians would reject chrematistics, especially when they pray "give us this day our daily bread" and do not ask for all the bread in the world.

Large business corporations in banking, food production, energy, and retailing, among others, thrive in the context of the market economy with its denial of limits. Their growth is dependent on the availability of natural resources, and their needless growth is also using up these resources. Richard Heinberg reports that the petro-geologist M. K. Hubbert was aware of the mismatch between our money system and the energy system. Our money system grows as money is loaned into circulation by the Federal Reserve Bank, and it has to grow continually in order to pay interest on the loans. Thus the need for economic growth is intrinsic to the money system itself. The mis-match occurs when there is no longer enough energy to facilitate the growth in the money system. When this occurs there will very likely be a serious financial crisis. (18) And if anthropologists are correct to postulate a correlation between the evolution of culture and the amount of energy used per capita, we would face a cultural devolution—the end of progress. The glamour of large corporations, which people like to emulate, would evaporate. They will not be our models in the future, if they exist at all. But they have made their money at the expense of the rest of us and will very likely seek to transform money into power over the rest of us for some time. Because they embody the denial of limits most completely and arrogate absolute power to themselves, I have come to think of these multi-national corporations as demonic structures. On the other hand, because they have insulated themselves from feedback by their arrogation of unconditional power, they fail to recognize that their power is not sustainable on social or ecological grounds. Their absolute power is their fatal weakness. Whereas the Faust legend portrayed the effects of demonic power on an individual level, multi-national corporations, with the protection of the United States empire in a fascist system, are demonstrating the effects of demonic power in a global system.

Many of us are so caught up in a "consensus trance," (a term that Erik Davis borrowed from psychologist Charles Tart to express the power of cultural presuppositions and social programming to shape our outlook,) (19) that we do not question the policies of big business. Very few of us may sense that large corporations are demonic structures as they shape our cultural presuppositions. Having grown accustomed to the notion that business responds to public demands, or that it provides for our needs, we often fail to recognize and question corporate activity that is not in the public interest. We forget that the first motivation of corporate activity is to make money. It will serve the people only if it can make money doing so. A current example is the use of nuclear power to generate electricity. Already in 1989 the cost of generating electricity with wind power was 6.4 cents per kilowatt hour, while nuclear power cost almost twice as much, 12.5 cents per kilowatt hour. (20) By now wind power is even more economical. Lester Brown reported that wind can be produced for less than 4 cents per kilowatt hour. (21) Why then does the nuclear industry still garner vastly more money for research than renewable energy and continue to propose more nuclear plants? Obviously they have the lobbying power, not to mention the synergy between the nuclear power and nuclear bombs. It is in their interest even though the public would have to pay twice as much for electricity—and bear the risk of a catastrophic nuclear accident. It was our outrage over such egregious greed that prompted my wife and I to build a house that is off the grid and depends entirely on the renewable energy of wind and sun for electricity and hot water.

It would be easy to list other examples of how corporations often serve their own interests at public expense. In order to generate profit corporations use advertising to persuade people to consume more and more things they do not really need. They also create more economic growth by transforming more and more goods that people had produced for themselves into commodities that people must buy. The market economy is very effective in doing this, growing at the expense of the household or non-monetized economy. This is especially true for food commodities and, as we shall see, it has spread to developing countries. With the help of fossil fuels food can be produced in enormous and affordable quantities. But what will happen to people who have been driven from productive land by corporate power after the fossil fuel subsidy is gone and the energy-intensive industrial methods of food production no longer work? Because such corporate greed is without limits it is inherently demonic and its evil effects are seen in its social irresponsibility.

All this is prompted by the desire for profit. According to a Biblical admonition, the love of money is the root of all evil (II Timothy 6: 10). This would seem to apply to a personal desire and, although corporations have gained protection under the Bill of Rights as "persons," which we recognize as a legal fiction, they also are driven by the quest for profit. During 2006, according to news reports, Exxon-Mobil enjoyed net profits of around 20 billion dollars, record profits because of the high price of oil. Exxon-Mobil seems to want money more than the good will of their customers as they play out their role in the oil endgame. And because Exxon-Mobil apparently recognizes no limits in its quest for profit, we recognize its demonic character. If money retains its viability after the end of oil, it will give them the power to be a player in the post-petroleum future.

The concept of the demonic, which had been rejected by the ideologues of progress and discarded by liberal religious thinkers as a medieval superstition, was revived early in the twentieth century by theologians such as Paul Tillich as religious thought was shaken by totalitarian regimes, by the barbarism of two World Wars, and especially by the social and ecological ravages of an unbridled capitalism driven by irrational acquisitiveness. More recently the theologian, David Ray Griffin, has offered an understanding of the demonic which is based on the philosophy of Alfred North Whitehead. In this view the demonic is the result of free human creativity as it creates cultural forms. But eventually the demonic may appear to us as a trans-human agency as it confronts us in the form of corporate or military power. Thus the demonic can be understood as "symbolic structures that channel human creativity toward destructive activities based on hate or indifference" (22) Griffin lists three aspects of the American Empire that show it, no less than the now-defunct Soviet Union, as an evil or demonic empire. First, even after the Soviet threat collapsed, military spending and preparedness in this country increased. Second, The United States continues to build nuclear weapons while self-righteously trying to restrain others, such as Iran, from doing so. Third, the Bush Administration, pressured by the oil corporations, refuses to curtail the emissions of carbon dioxide as this country burns more fossil fuels than any other country. With only 5 % of the worlds population, the United States generates 33% of its carbon dioxide. These actions of the United States, driven by the desire for limitless profit and power, are threats to the survival of all life on the planet. Christians, who treasure the earth as God's good creation, should be up in arms over such malfeasance. But they too are victimized by demonic symbolic structures and kept in a trance.

This new awareness of the demonic in and through secular activities can also help us recognize the demonic dimension of our cultural fixation on money. The pursuit of money is often a means of gaining power; hence the equation "money is power." The desire to make money is certainly not innocent, and when this desire is insatiable, its moral value and psychological origins are ambiguous. Even secular corporations, managed by people who like to make money for shareholders who also want to make money, are involved in the dialectic of the divine and the demonic.

Norman O. Brown on the Demonic
This dialectic of divine and demonic energy is developed in Norman O. Brown's Freudian analysis of cultural dynamics. He explains that the secular affirmation of making money is a dialectical negation of the sacred (not a simple

or absolute negation) which affirms what it negates in a distorted form. "Modern secularism," wrote Brown, "and its companion Protestantism, do not usher in an era in which human consciousness is liberated from inhuman powers, or the natural world is liberated from supernatural manifestations; the essence of the Protestant (or capitalist) era is that the power over the world has passed from God to God's negation, God's ape, the Devil. And already Luther had seen in money the essence of the secular, and therefore of the demonic. The money complex is the demonic, and the demonic is God's ape; the money complex is therefore the heir to and substitute for the religious complex, an attempt to find God in things." (23) *Notice that Brown is using mythic imagery here in a metaphorical way to uncover the psycho-religious roots of the market economy as the driving force in industrial societies.*

We have reviewed several understanding of demonic power in our world: first, it is the denial of limits as corporations, with governmental protection, engage in self-aggrandizing activity while disregarding the welfare of all others. Second, these structures are demonic as they render the earth, God's good creation, unfit for human habitation. Third, we have seen how the demonic is a symbolic structure in our culture that keeps many of us in a "cultural trance" so that we do not object to the exercise of demonic power. Many of us are "demon-possessed" in this sense.

The Market Economy and the Enclosure of the Commons

To understand the centrality of the money complex we must remember how the market economy evolved as the pre-eminent activity in industrial societies. This story was told by economic historian Karl Polanyi in *The Great Transformation*. Polanyi began by explaining that the emergence of the market economy during the industrial revolution was a truly unique event. Prior to this, according to historical and anthropological research, although there were local markets, the economy of people was submerged in or merely an aspect of their social relationships. The great transformation that culminated during the nineteenth century was that "instead of economy being embedded in social relations, social relations are embedded in the conomic system." (24) This disembedded economy was now free from social or moral constraints or limitations. It was free to grow, and it did so by gradually replacing the household economy and informal small markets with the market economy in which commodities were produced and sold for money. Social mores and ethical considerations were swept aside as the demand for profit took precedence.

Along with the centrality of money, Polanyi also mentions the importance of machines which made the production of commodities possible. The producer of commodities, the manufacturer, requires a supply of raw materials, including energy, and workers. or a labor force. In the context of the market economy, "machine production in a commercial society involves, in effect, no less a transformation than that of the natural and human substance of society into commodities." (25) Thus the industrial mode of production has transformed human beings and nature into resources for production, and in the process it uses them up. Natural resources, which had been the common property of people, had to be "enclosed."

The processes of enclosure and commodification began with a series of "Enclosure Acts" in 17th and 18th century England. These acts more or less legally allowed the lords and nobles to "enclose" their land holdings and thereby to expel the peasants who had lived on their lands. For many generations prior to this the land had been considered as a "commons" which provided subsistence for the peasants and a small income to the lords and nobles. With the growth of markets for wool the land owners realized they could make more profit by enclosing or fencing their land for the grazing of sheep. The expelled peasants moved to cities where some of them found work as laborers in the factories that were emerging as the industrial revolution began. The Enclosure Acts can be considered as the archetypal processes in which the "commons" are transformed into "resources" for the production of commodities. The world-view of corporate industrialism is now so total that few citizens in advanced industrial societies are aware of the theft of the commons. This wholesale theft is another reflection of the demonic refusal to accept self-limitation. We have learned to accept the fact that the resources that had been our common property will be used to produce the goods we think we need. The best we can do is to hope and urge that these resources will be used in a frugal and careful manner.

The costs of commodification are several. As the market economy grows at the expense of the household economy the industrial process places a heavy demand on scarce resources, such as oil, and adds to the burden of pollution. Barry Commoner gave many examples of "technological displacement" as a natural or organic product (soap) was replaced by a synthetic product (detergent). Another example: "Like an addictive drug, fertilizer nitrogen and synthetic pesticides literally create increased demand as they are used; the buyer becomes hooked on the product." (26) The economy gains at the expense of ecology. An even greater cost is the loss of subsistence activities. As a homesteader, trying to be self-reliant in food production, I was aware of this and our School of Homesteading was designed to help young people recover the arts and skills of raising and processing food at home. But as I studied the writings of Ivan Illich I was made aware of the more important implications of this process. Because we no longer even have a word for such subsistence activities, Illich proposed the word "vernacular." (27) We still use this word for the language we learn at home versus the language we were taught in school. But originally the word "vernacular" referred to a wider range of activities or things produced at home for use at home. It is thus the opposite of commodities, goods or services we purchase.

The loss of vernacular competence may prove to be the most tragic loss humans will suffer as commodities gain a "radical monopoly" over the satisfaction of human needs. Illich coined the term "radical monopoly" to mean "the subsitution of an industrial product or professional service for a useful activity in which people engage or would like to engage." (28) At some point, Illich argued, the radical monopoly of industrial goods or services destroys the possible synergy that might have been possible between vernacular products and commodities. This will be ever more important as we move toward the constraints that shortages of oil will impose on industrial production. Vast numbers of people have lost the ability to be self-reliant.

It is wise to remember that what we refer to as development is essentially the process of commodification—getting people to buy manufactured goods. Development is a process that creates winners and losers. Losers are those who lose the opportunities for vernacular activities but do not have enough money to buy commodities. This situation was obvious to scholars who studied the effects of transnational corporations, such as Richard Barnet. He expected a "world employment crisis of horrendous proportions . . . . The process of industrialization in the Third World is taking place almost automatically. The pace differs from country to country, but the basic social effects are much the same. The subsistence economy in which money w as rarely used . . . is being sucked into the international money economy" (29) Displaced from the land, peasants and small farmers flock to cities where job-displacing technology in factories offer jobs to very few. Thus slums are growing around cities all over the world. The results are that there are many more losers than winners, a fact seen in the growing disparity in income. The top fifth of the world's people receives 82.7% of total world income, while the bottom three fifths receives 5.4%. The second fifth from the top, the world's middle classes, receive 11.7% but are gradually falling into the lower classes. (30) This was in 1992. The disparity in income has grown since then. In this country, according to Gar Alperwitz, "the top 1 percent has twice the income as the bottom 100 million Americans." (31)

Because the corporations that rule the world refuse to acknowledge limits, they are "enclosing" more than land, which they now achieve through economic pressure rather than government edict. Corporate media have enclosed the air waves for profitable broadcast. Air and water are being enclosed and transformed into resources for industrial production or as sinks for industrial waste. In some areas water is polluted and those who can afford it get water purifiers. Others turn to bottled water. What had been common property is enclosed in bottles and made a commodity. The poor drink polluted tap water. Ground water, which had been a commons, is now depleted in many areas by irrigation.

One of the more flagrant examples of enclosure in our time is the patenting of seeds and plants. Farmers had been selecting and improving seed varieties for centuries. The introduction of hybrids mark the beginning of a new dependency on purchased seed since seeds from hybrids produce inferior crops. Now, with the establishment of intellectual property rights, genetically-modified seeds are patented and farmers who use them have to pay a royalty to the seed company. The seeds that had been the common property of indigenous populations for centuries have been enclosed. Herman Daly and John Cobb comment on this "troubling possibility": "To imagine the common heritage of all life, the gene pool, being taken over as private property is the culmination of individualistic economics, and the ultimate negation of community." (32) Finally, global warming is the "enclosure" of the atmosphere as a sink for carbon dioxide.

How Could our Cultural Values Change?

This review of dysfunctional values that undergird our culture of exuberance is surely getting tedious. It is time to summarize. Where have we gone wrong? We have explored the roots of the ideology of progress in the Western notion of sacred history, the quest for knowledge and the technological power to improve on nature, the ambiguous quest for money as a measure of progress, and our acceptance of corporate-controlled industrialism for the production of the things we think we need. More specifically, we have yielded to the seductions of consumerism. We have thereby given our consent and support to the corporations that have thereby grown powerful enough to control our government and transform it from a democracy to a plutocracy. Thus the Empire, which may have been embyronic in America from the outset, emerged in full force. And, to enhance economic growth the multinational corporations are working to destroy self-reliant activities all around the globe. All these factors are deeply rooted in our history and reinforced by cultural values. It is easy to see the list of values that constitute the American Dream as a series of mutually reinforcing factors. American history has been, in the terminology of systems thinkers, a series of positive feedback loops that have reinforced the culture of exuberance. How can we possibly imagine that our cultural values would change?

One way that has been the topic of many books and articles such as those titled "100 Ways You Can Save the Planet," is to make changes in personal lifestyle. Although this is necessary it is not sufficient, but it continues to be the emphasis in popular environmental handbooks. Even Evangelical Christians, many of whom affirm environmental attitudes under the rubric of "Creation Care," are getting on this bandwagon as illustrated by a recent book, *Serve God, Save the Planet*. The author, a medical doctor, emphasizes the good things each of us can do in the way we live. "To trust that government or science will fix everything is to abdicate our personal roles as stewards. One of the key features of Christianity is its emphasis on a personal God, personal redemption, and personal accountability. We cannot depend on the state, our church, or science to redeem us today or in the afterlife." (33) This emphasis on personal responsibility is consistent with the Christian emphasis on personal salvation, which was discussed in Chapter I, but in this chapter we have seen how our environmental problems are deeply rooted in our culture and caused by institutional momentum beyond personal choices. Personal decisions are necessary and important, but without institutional changes they are insufficient and ultimately ineffective. Therefore we need to be emphasizing a combination of personal action and political responsibility as we move into the changing social context created by rising energy prices.

We can see some evidence that America is on the cusp of cultural change. There are already many dissatisfactions with American culture, some vague and others more definite. There are the economic disparities mentioned earlier which a few recognize as a clear threat. For others these are more vague as they continue to identify with the rich and vote for policies that benefit the rich even though they are impoverished thereby. Then there are the various forms of pollution which are increasingly undeniable even though it seems to be a national policy to export polluting industries as much as possible. There are vague discontents about the lack of spiritual fulfillment as material affluence continues as expressed in Paul Wachtel's book, *The Poverty of Affluence*. Then there was the energy crisis of the Seventies which, while it was dismissed by the majority, definitely challenged the optimism of some. I know this for a fact, since I was one of these. And there are vague feelings of anxiety about the fact that our country has been saddled with a national debt of around nine trillion dollars.

As I write now, in 2008, one of the clearer dissatisfactions in our society is triggered by gradually rising energy prices. As a culture we may be on the verge of recognizing that our energy legacy was a one-time gift. We will soon recognize that the energy-rich twentieth century was an anomaly in human history. When this becomes clear to most of us it will constitute a massive negative feedback loop which will challenge the values of the exuberant culture. The second negative feedback loop may very likely be the beginnings of climate change as storms get more violent and weather patterns become less reliable and the ocean levels rise. These events may also, of course, trigger even more violent cultural upheavals, but the best we can expect from them are deep shifts in the kind of thinking that had sustained the American Dream. As more and more people recognize what we have done to our planet, we see that the planet is vulnerable to human actions. This recognition can lead to a reversal of the traditional view in Western Civilization which has promoted the conquest and domination of nature as a hostile power. Even evangelical Christians are, as they recognize the threat of global warming, expressing concern about the preservation of the planet. Thus our culture as a whole can move to a recognition that we must protect Mother Earth, and this recognition is reinforced by business interests led by the insurance industry. As ocean levels rise, cities are at risk around the world, and a global consensus on the need to reduce greenhouse gases is emerging. As these events are clarified by books like this, by many more effective modes of communication, and by daily experience, it is entirely predictable that American values will indeed change. But the way out of the grasp of Empire will not be easy. It will require practical solutions, as outlined in the next chapter, reinforced by a set of earth-centered spiritual values.

We can take comfort in the fact that earth-centered spiritual values are emerging again out of the recessive genes in our cultural organism. From the time of Thomas Jefferson onwards, there has been a strong agrarian tradition in America. It has defined itself as the opposite of the industrial ethos. One of its most articulate proponents has been Wendell Berry and in recent years other voices have joined in calling for locally-raised organic food and self-reliant modes of activity. In contrast to the dominant strand in the American experience, which thrives on the denial of limits, the agrarian tradition recognizes limits. As Wendell Berry put it, "agrarian farmers see, accept, and live within their limits." (34)

Another pulse of earth-centered spirituality is emerging out of the counter-culture of the 60s and 70s. Some of these have been developing into powerful currents of cultural transformation, and they are reviewed in Chapters VII and VIII below. According to sociologist Paul Ray and Sherry Ruth Anderson, these movements add up to over 50 million people they call Cultural and Spiritual Creatives. (35) This is a third sub-culture in America, in addition to the "moderns" and the "traditionals" who broke away from the "moderns" earlier. Cultural Creatives broke away from the "moderns" mainly during the past fifty years and their numbers continue to grow. If Cultural Creatives can stand up to the power vested in our political and economic institutions, as they were reviewed in this chapter, they may be the vanguard of change if and when they discover their political power. We shall return to a more detailed review of Cultural Creatives in the final chapter.

Meanwhile, the world needs a kind of transition strategy so it can begin a gradual and equitable reduction in oil consumption. Apart from international agreements there would be an anarchistic competition between nations for the remaining oil. Plans for such agreement exist, and in a recent book Richard Heinberg evaluates them and proposes especially a protocol based on the rate at which global oil production declines: "signatory nations would agree to reduce their oil consumption gradually and uniformly according to a simple formula that works out to being a little less than three percent per year." (36) Although other plans are based on reducing the rate of emissions of carbon dioxide in order to mitigate the process of global warming, Heinberg believes that a plan based on the rate of oil depletion is more urgent and would also reduce emissions. Needless to say, the implementation of any such international plan would require a great deal of negotiation in order to work out the details and assure fairness and equity between nations. Thus there are alternatives to international chaos and anarchy at the time of the end of oil. Alternatives such as the oil depletion protocol would provide an orderly way down from total dependence on oil and promote the development of other sources of energy. The big question is whether the United States, with its imperial ambitions and a population addicted to oil, can adapt to using less oil.

CHAPTER III

CHANGES NEEDED AS WE
ADAPT TO THE END OF OIL

A List of Needed Changes

The following list of needed changes illustrates the magnitude of the problem as we seek a culture that would help people adapt to a new age of scarcity. The list is given here in its entirety to help us see the range of issues at a glance; later each issue will be elucidated further. I have tried to list the kinds of changes that can occur through both the personal and political initiatives of people. The powers that be, government and corporations, are usually invested in keeping things as they are, as the Bush administration has been resisting a shift to renewable energy. We the people are colonized by those powers, and it should go without saying that needed changes could be greatly facilitated by a process of decolonization, especially in relation to issues involving economics, energy or technology.

From linear history to cyclical return.
From anthropocentrism to biocentrism.
From economic growth to a steady state economy.
From demonic acquisitiveness to the distrust of money.
From commodities to vernacular activities.
From industrial technology to appropriate technology.
From enclosure to liberation of the commons.
From the domination of nature to cooperation with nature in food production.
From centralized control to decentralized local control.
From non-renewable fossil fuels to renewable sources of energy.

From Linear History to Cyclical Return

This topic is elucidated in one of the most popular and influential of Mircea Eliade's books: *Cosmos and History: The Myth of the Eternal Return.* This book, which has been very influential among literate readers generally, is also interesting as we see how this great historian of religion pushes the limits of scholarly objectivity as he repeatedly warns of the "terror of history" and of the existential difficulties of historicism as a worldview. History is a terror for people who suffer its consequences, such as anxiety over nuclear war or ecological devastation or the end of oil. It is only the few people in power who can "make" history; the rest of us are its victims. As long as Christianity was a viable religious possibility people could tolerate this terror by faith in the God who acted in history and somehow directed those who made history. Surely there are still some people who live by faith in this manner, but, as was pointed out in the previous chapter, the concept of sacred history has disintegrated into secular history which some still value as the locus of endless technological progress. In the post-petroleum age this too will lose its prestige and pass away.

In contrast to the terror of history, Eliade offers a vision of eternal cyclical return drawn mainly from archaic (or "primitive") religions. The main focus was on the myths and rituals connected to the new year. By a ritual reenactment of the primordial chaos that preceded the creation of the world, the world is allowed to die annually and then, by ritually repeating the cosmogonic act, (the act that created the world), the world, and time, is recreated. Many of us still repeat debased versions of this: drunken chaos on New Year's Eve, followed by resolutions on New Year's Day, which is symbolized by a baby. In archaic societies, according to Eliade, the New Year's rituals annually abolished and recreated time so that it was not allowed to accumulate and become history. Eliade speculates that as ecological devastation and the nuclear peril add to the terror of history human culture might seek to "prohibit" the events of history by a reintegration of human societies into a world shaped only by the repetition of archaic archetypes. We shall explore this very real possibility in chapter VIII.

Structures of cyclical time recur throughout the history of religion. The Sun Dance of the Plains Indians in this country was held annually at the time of the summer solstice, at the time when the sun was strongest so that a new earth would be recreated. Cyclical time is proposed here as an alternative to history and progress and because it is congruent with a life lived closer to the procession of the seasons. Wendell Berry has most eloquently expressed this relationship between religion and farming and cyclical return. He explains that farming is "a practical religion, a practice of religion, a rite. By farming we enact our fundamental connection with energy and matter, light and darkness. In the cycles of farming, which carry the elemental energy again and again through the seasons and the bodies of living things, we recognize the only infinitude within reach of the imagination." (1) Also, while cyclical time may allow hope that the coming year will be better than the past year, it does not encourage progress or long-term hope for technological solutions that fail to work out and end in disappointment. Thus cyclical time facilitates a kind of fatalistic contentment.

From Anthropocentrism to Biocentrism.

In a biocentric vision humans see themselves as fellow-citizens with non-humans in an earth community. All forms of life have intrinsic value and humans have no right to harm other forms of life in ways other than necessary participation in the food chain. We also need to be clear about what biocentrism does not say. First, it does not deny that humans have become the dominant species on the earth in terms of power to change the earth. Biocentric deep ecologists, however, do express much disapproval of the growth in human population, based as it is on the exploitation of other life-forms, and urge steps toward the reduction of population so there is room for fellow creatures. Second, biocentrism does not deny the process of human self-transcendence, or self-reflective consciousness. Humans (at least some of them) thereby understand the problems they have caused on the earth and seek to remedy them. In this respect human consciousness has placed humans "above" other animals. Thus biocentrism does not imply that humans should abdicate responsibility. John Cobb has grappled with these issues in relation to the thought of Paul Shepherd, a radical deep ecology thinker. Shepherd urged that we humans should renounce our self-transcendence because our actions as managers of the planet have been so bad. Cobb responded that "it is only by the most radical self-transcendence that he (Shepherd) has come to the insight as to the immensely destructive role of self-transcendence in the history of this planet." (2) It is thus only through self-transcendence that we can recognize the value of a biocentric orientation.

Anthropocentrism, as it has elevated and thus isolated the human over other life forms, has diminished the possibility of full human self-realization since this is possible only through our human relationship with other life forms. Thus, as deep ecology thinkers argue, biocentrism leads to a more comprehensive self-realization. (3) We have also learned, thanks to people like Rachel Carson whose book, *Silent Spring*, helped to bring about ecological awareness when it was published in 1962, that efforts to control nature usually have blow-back effects that are harmful to the human environment. She ended her book with these words: "The 'control of nature' is a phrase conceived in arrogance, born in the Neanderthal age of biology and philosophy, when it was supposed that nature exists for the convenience of man. The concepts and practices of applied entomology for the most part date from that Stone Age of science. It is our alarming misfortune that so primitive a science has armed itself with the most modern and terrible weapons, and that in turning them against the insects it has also turned them against the earth." This is a fair description of anthropocentrism and its effects.

Perhaps some would argue that, given the fact that males have initiated much of the destruction of earth's ecosystem, that this section should have been titled "from androcentrism to biocentrism." Feminist writers emphasize the ago-old association of women and nature and charge men with the exploitation of both. This continues to the present day, and as Carolyn Merchant showed, it was especially vicious at the outset of the scientific revolution and in the development of technology as a mechanistic worldview replaced an organic worldview and led to the death of nature. Men seem to find it easier to abstract themselves from their bodies and to use them, along with the rest of the natural world, in their effort to gain control. One sign of hope may be that as energy becomes scarce and expensive, men will find it more difficult to control nature. If the end of cheap oil leads to the end of the industrial isolation of the human from nature, it may open the possibility that we can live on more intimate terms with non-human animals. Apart from factory farms, many people do this already. When I maintained a small herd of dairy cows during the 1980s, I got to know each of them and their idiosyncrasies quite well. I brought them into the barn for milking and feeding twice a day and cared for them when they needed help at birthing or when they were sick. While they are not our intellectual equals, they are creatures of deep feeling and extremely sensitive to the nuances of feeling we express in actions or tones of voice.

As for confinement of animals on factory farms, I believe it is wrong and I never kept farm animals that way. Nor is cruelty ever justifiable. But I did keep farm animals and sometimes slaughtered them for food. This runs counter to those in the animal rights movement who believe we should not kill and eat animals. I have known many people who disagree with me on this and I respect their choices. But as an environmentalist I am more concerned to preserve the species than individuals, and I recognize the reality of food chains and predation in animal communities. I do also respect the relationship people develop with pets, special individuals of a species, and recognize it is important for those people. But I cannot agree that this is a moral principle that should be normative. Many small-scale farmers and homesteaders keep goats or a cow for milk and chickens for eggs. Males of these species usually provide meat for the family or are sold for a bit of income. As homesteader Carla Emery once wrote: we feed them and they feed us. And on the small homestead where animals usually find food on land that is not suitable for raising crops that could be fed to humans, and where their wastes provide fertility for the soil, farm animals do not take food from humans. In brief, although sentimentality about individual animals or pets is a good way for people to relate to the non-human world, is not a necessity in a biocentric orientation. This is especially critical for people who are trying to live within natural energy flows, as people do when they live on the land and eat the food they raise rather than food from the industrial food system. Fishing and hunting for game could similarly be part of a biocentric orientation. This rationale for eating animals does not deny that one might feel guilt over doing so, as I and many of my friends on the farm admit. Ritual acknowledgement of this guilt helped to propitiate it for archaic hunters. and such rituals would be good for all of us, since we all do participate in the cycle of life and death.

From Economic Growth to a Steady-State Economy.

Some readers may feel that the topics in this and subsequent sections in this chapter are becoming more and more esoteric. Actually, they deal with fairly ordinary topics such as economic growth, money and debt, and commodities, but they do so in unconventional ways. As we face unprecedented circumstances at the end of cheap oil, it will be helpful to begin thinking outside of the box. Readers are therefore urged to be patient and open-minded.

Given the fact that the environmental problems caused by unchecked economic growth have been referred to repeatedly in this book, along with evidence that such growth can not continue indefinitely, especially as oil becomes scarce and expensive, there is no need to present additional reasons why it is prudent to think about a steady-state economy. It is important to think about it and plan for it on a cultural level so that it may be possible to merge gracefully into a future when lack of resources such as oil will curtail economic growth. To do this we need some understanding of what is implied by the phrase "steady-state economy," and we shall attempt to get this primarily from the work of Herman Daly. Daly has been working on this topic since the early Seventies, even before the first energy crisis. A few other economists have joined in promoting a steady-state economy. Kenneth Boulding, with his masterful use of imagery, contrasted the cowboy, who roams over a vast and open range to exploit, to the spaceman, who lives in the closed system of the spaceship and thus symbolized a steady-state economy. Daly recognizes that the idea of steady-state economics represents a paradigm shift in economic thought and that most economists are still working with the old paradigm which denies limits to growth. "Orthodox growth economics, as we have seen, recognizes that particular resources are limited but does not recognize any general scarcity of all resources together. The orthodox dogma is that technology can always substitute new resources for old, without limit." (4) This is the old argument that higher prices will "find" more resources, but who can afford to pay higher prices? Certainly not most people in the world, and not most of us.

This brings us to another big lie told by advocates of growth. It was summarized by President Kennedy when he said that a rising tide lifts all ships. Since then Reagonomics gave us the "trickle-down" theory. How is it then that as economic growth has prevailed in recent years there has been increasing economic inequality? The rich get richer and the poor get poorer, both between countries and within our country. It seems to be a zero-sum game with not enough goodies to go around. Daly distinguishes between a steady-state economy and a failed growth economy which occurs in times of economic recession. He points out that limited resources would eventually cause growth to fail, and that it would be better to plan for that by a deliberate policy of curtailing growth. Without such planning, recessions are times of unemployment and suffering, such as we had during the last energy crisis and will have during the coming energy crisis. Also, a transition to steady-state economics, which would very likely curtail jobs, must be accompanied by other forms of work than traditional employment, an issue we shall discuss presently.

A steady-state economy is defined as a constant population of human bodies and a constant supply of stock, which could include artifacts or capital assets adequate to provide a good life for the human population for a long time. There is also a through-put of matter and energy needed to maintain the population and the stock. This is to be kept at the lowest feasible rate, and the artifacts are designed for long life and durability. There is no limit on intangible items such as technology, information, wisdom, goodness, and so forth. (5) Thus a steady-state economy need not be a stagnant culture. There is plenty of room for competition, for example, as people find ways of using less energy for more services, or less material for better artifacts. Thus a steady state might represent the end of progress when progress is thought of as economic growth, or acquisition of wealth, but it is not the end of cultural progress.

A caveat is in order here. When our work is no longer done by oil, it may be that our culture will not have as much time to devote to scientific inquiry or cultural enrichment. It is easy to underestimate how much free time we enjoy as a result of our energy slaves. For example, a gallon of gasoline, burned in an internal combustion engine at 20% efficiency, still produces the equivalent of 6200 kilocalories of work. Or, as David and Marcia Pimentel explained further, "one gallon of gasoline produces work equivalent to 97 manpower hours, or one man working eight hours a day, five days a week for about 2.5 weeks." (6) Without the time for inquiry that these energy slaves make possible, it might be wise to recognize that after cheap oil there may also be some reductions in the acquisition of knowledge. (7) This may be a good thing since new knowledge invites practical application and we may not yet have the wisdom to discern which applications are useful and which are not. We shall return to this topic in the next chapter.

Daly discusses a variety of social institutions and strategies that might help to bring a steady-state economy into being. Most depend on policies that politicians would have to vote on. But, just as economic growth is stimulated by an abundance of cheap energy, so expensive energy will discourage growth. As theologian Karl E. Peters suggested, when cheap energy is not available, "the society's values may change toward those of a steady state, such as conservation, the maintenance of traditions and stability." (8) Peters goes on to say that if there is change it is likely to be cyclical change associated with the seasons of nature.

To stabilize population, so births are equal to deaths, some birth control measures are necessary. Daly mentions a possibility suggested by Kenneth Boulding: transferable birth licenses, of which each woman would receive two and a tenth. These could be sold or given to others or inherited in case the woman dies. Others have proposed other plans, most of which are coercive. (9) Some plans depend on abortion, which the Religious Right currently considers a sin and is trying to make into a crime. Surely it is no less sinful than to require every baby to be born to women who have already been impoverished and are increasingly denied the assistance they need to raise that child up to healthy citizenship—all by a government of that same Religious Right! Such tactics, along with the power of the prevailing growth paradigm, supported by its deep cultural roots in the millenary vision of progress, do not encourage us to see an early change to a steady-state economy. But we must also notice a growing disenchantment with affluence, represented by book titles such as *The Overworked American: The Unexpected Decline in Leisure, The Loss of Happiness in Market Democracies, The Joyless Economy, Wealth Addiction, The Harried Leisure Class, The Poverty of Affluence, The Culture of Narcissism.* (by Juliet Schor, Robert Lane, Tibor Scitovsky, Philip Slater, Steffan Linder, Paul Wachtel, and Christopher Lasch, respectively). Perhaps here, as in so many other areas, it is the people who will lead. We can only hope that the leaders will follow.

So far we have considered the possibility of a steady state only in the United States. On a global level the issue is more complex and difficult, especially in relation to population growth. Graphs which show the J-curve of rising energy use also show a similar J-curve to represent the growth of population. At this point the issue of carrying capacity and possible die-off raises its ugly head. Programs that could curtail birth rates where they are still higher than death rates should be implemented immediately.

From Demonic Acquisitiveness to the Distrust of Money.

By "demonic acquisitiveness" we mean the effort to make unlimited amounts of money. Aristotle, who recognized this as an unnatural perversion, called it "chrematistics" in distinction from "oikonomia," or household management. My reasons for calling it a demonic activity were given in the previous chapter. In the context of our consideration of a steady-state economy, we can add that the ideology of unlimited economic growth is demonic because is postulates exponential growth in its money system because of compound interest. On the one hand, money functions as a medium of exchange, and as such is a useful invention. But the way money is created by being loaned into existence, on the other hand, raises serious problems about money.

Money originates from the Federal Reserve System, which loans it out and collects interest on it. Commercial banks, of course, also "create" money when they make loans. Herman Daly and Joshua Farley point out that "over 90% of our money supply today is not currency but demand deposits created by the private commercial banking system." (10) This requires growth in the system as a whole so that there is money to pay the interest; it is a built-in incentive for economic growth. But there cannot be infinite exponential growth in a finite system, and the earth and its resources are finite. A German writer, Margrit Kennedy, argues that any capital-intensive production of goods or services will cost, on the average, twice as much as necessary because of the cost of interest. (11) Every kind of interest is an efficient mechanism for the transfer of wealth from the poor to the rich. Thus the money system has been the economic mechanism leading to the world-wide disparity of income. Griffin and others have called this "global apartheid" as a minority of white people have appropriated vastly more of the world's wealth than the majority of poor people who suffer as a result. The economic policies of the American Empire, usually called "development," continue to increase this disparity: "In 1960 people in the richest fifth were thirty times wealthier than the poorest fifth. By 1997 they had become 74 times wealthier." (12) Griffin correctly sees this as the exercise of demonic power.

Interest, which should cover the costs involved in making a loan, if any, is a nicer term to describe money paid for the use of money than usury, which is condemned by most of the world's religions. We can notice in passing that this reinforces the demonic dimension of the acquisition of money. Usury usually implies an excessive rate of interest, as in the case of credit card debt. In any case, the rate of economic growth in the system as a whole must be equal to the average rate of interest, so that the interest can be paid. But, as mentioned above, exponential growth cannot be sustained in a finite system. So far population growth and industrialism have allowed enough economic expansion so mask the destructive effects of interest. Margrit Kennedy points out that countries like the United States have been making loans to developing countries to keep the system going, though many of these loans will not be repaid. (13) Ecological limits to economic growth and population growth are at hand. Another evidence of limits is the increasing transfer of wealth from poor to rich people. Still another is the growing national debt, now estimated at around 9 trillion dollars, which adds to the interest to be paid. But the decisive factor which will destroy this "grow or die" financial system is the end of cheap oil. The mis-match between the money system and the energy system, already noticed by M. K. Hubbert, was mentioned above in the preceding chapter. Daly and Farley quote Hubbert on "exponential growth as a transient phenomenon in human history." (14) When the high price of oil will limit economic growth, the federal money system will not serve all the people without local systems.

Fortunately there are programs of complementary currencies on local levels which could work in tandem with the money systems created by banks. It is on these that books by Margrit Kennedy, Thomas Greco and Bernard Lietaer are focused. Most of these are small local systems of "mutual credit." The most popular of these are "Local Employment and Trading Systems" (LETS), originated by a Canadian, Michael Linton in 1983. LETSystems have been started in a few progressive communities in this country, more in Canada, and many in other countries. My wife and I started such as system in our small town of 2000 and it worked for a couple of years, but it eventually failed because, with only about 20 members, we probably did not have a "critical mass" of participants. 50 to 100 would be a better size for a LETSystem. This is essentially a multi-lateral barter system in which members "buy" or "sell" goods or services to each other and report the transaction to a record-keeper. Buyer and seller agree on the price and report it as a credit or debit but do not pay or receive cash. Members list the goods or services they offer or want in a newsletter or on a website. Greco explains the finer points of a LETSystem and evaluates some of its problems. (15)

Other local systems of mutual credit include local currencies, such as the Ithaca "hours" or the Berkshire "shares," or Boulder "hours." The most comprehensive overview of these local complementary currencies, along with strong arguments for their necessity, is found in Lietaer's work. (16) *http://www.berkshares.org)*. During the Great Depression of the Thirties there were many attempts to offer such a local currency, or scrip, systems in this country and in Europe. Many failed and some were restricted by law after successfully competing with the official money system. A LETSystem is not illegal, and it has the advantage, along with local currencies, of making the equivalent of money free and available on a small-scale local level. It also helps to keep money circulating in the local community.

The important need for interest-free money is when people make a major purchase, such as a house. James Robertson has emphasized the need for a multi-level currency system, from local to international currencies so that none is at a competitive disadvantage. (17) Margrit Kennedy proposes that an interest-free money system in a country could be managed by charging a small "parking fee" to those who hold money (if they hold it out of circulation beyond a given time) instead of charging interest to people who need money. (18) This kind of system was originally proposed by Silvio Gesell at the end of the nineteenth century. It was tried during the Great Depression in the attempt to stimulate the economy by making money more freely available. Kennedy argued that even rich people who have made money by charging interest would agree to this if and when they felt that the money system was in jeopardy and they risk losing their principal. An interest-free money system would also avoid the inflation that usually emerges when government debt outgrows government income. If the end of cheap oil exacerbates this problem and places the money system at greater risk, an interest-free system should emerge as a political initiative—disguised, perhaps, as a very low interest rate. Many people distrust money already and more will in the future. A revised money system should also be accompanied by land reform, a topic we shall take up later in this chapter.

From Commodities to Vernacular Activities.

Still another way of avoiding the debt trap in the current money system is to spend less. We could do this in different ways. We can move out of a commodity-intensive way of life by working to understand and reject the way advertising induces us to buy more consumer goods. We can cultivate a life of voluntary simplicity as a positive incentive for a number of reasons, such as the Quaker way of living simply that others may simply live. We can avoid conspicuous consumption for environmental reasons by living lightly on the earth.

But once we clearly recognize that commodities, which we can buy with money, proliferated by replacing things people used to make for themselves, we can recover those vernacular activities. At a time in America when one on four meals is eaten in restaurants we have a simple illustration. Needless to say, spending less money also liberates us from having to make as much money. When my wife and I began raising and preserving our food, we were able to live comfortably on a teacher's half-salary. As a man who had full-time employment prior to then, it was enlightening for me to do what women had traditionally done—that is, unpaid work in the household economy. I have to admit that I also wanted to do this because I have always enjoyed the diversity and contrast between physical and mental activities.

As was mentioned earlier, one of the most insightful proponents of vernacular activities has been Ivan Illich, and he gave us the term "vernacular" to refer more broadly to that which is produced at home, like the language we learned at home compared to the language taught in school by professionals. This emphasis in the thought of Illich has been organized more coherently and systematically by a Peruvian architect/economist, Alfredo Lopez de Romana. He has called for the homecoming of economics which has, for too long, been out there serving the interests of industry and government. De Romana distinguishes between the formal/industrial sector and the informal/vernacular sphere, which has been nearly obliterated by the growth of the formal, money economy as it gained a radical monopoly on the satisfaction of human needs with commodities. Although the term "informal economy" is often applied to the non-monetized economy only, de Romana used it to refer to the realm in which people do odd jobs, small businesses, and community activities that require less capital and more ingenuity.

The vernacular realm of household and community activities has been parasitized by the market economy, which grows, in part, by displacing vernacular activities. As we thus become individualistic consumers of commodities, the social fabric is disintegrating. But De Romana is not proposing a return to preindustrial ways of life. Rather, he believes that "an extremely efficient synergy is possible between the formal and autonomous sectors, between the exchange economy and vernacular autoproduction." (19) As a prelude to this it is necessary to understand that the formal economy enjoys a parasitical relationship with the autonomous economy. Once this is recognized and the industrial economy has contracted, it may be possible to move toward a "post-crisis equilibrium." Perhaps the high price of oil will raise the cost of commodities to where vernacular activities and small-scale production in the informal economy are competitive. Another way of thinking about this new/old mode of human activity is with the terms popularized by James Robertson, who calls it "ownwork" in distinction from "outwork" or conventional employment which has been the form which work was given in the industrial era. (20)

Although we in the United States are already shifting into a post-industrial society as many manufacturing jobs are moving to countries where labor is cheaper, jobs in the service sector, at lower wages, keep many people employed. Local governments still provide incentives to attract business growth so there will be jobs, while policies that might facilitate more ownwork, or vernacular activities, are still not on the political radar screen. But as the cost of oil continues to rise and curtails industrial production, new alternatives will become visible. These may include more paid work in the informal, local economy as food production, for example, becomes more labor-intensive rather than energy-intensive, a possibility to be explored in coming sections. And for many people it will be more satisfying to do things than to have things as commodities. "Having," in itself, is not really fulfilling.

From Industrial Technology to Appropriate Technology.

Industrial modes of production expanded as fossil fuels, first coal, then oil and natural gas, became available. But just as it is impossible to conceive of industrialism without fossil fuels, so it is impossible to conceive of the industrial mode of production without cheap and available fossil fuels. Thanks to the work of E. F. Schumacher and many others, we can be confident that it will be possible to provide the goods and services we need after cheap fuels are no longer available. There was a vital "appropriate technology" movement several years ago and the insights that it made possible will be even more relevant in the coming years.

One of the first points to emphasize here is that technology is not, as many people like to think, morally neutral or value-free. Wendell Berry has reminded us of the complexity of technology: "Technology joins us to energy, to life. It is not, as many technologists would have us believe, a simple connection. Our technology is the practical aspect of our culture. By it we enact our religion, or our lack of it." (21) Fossil-fueled technology uses a precious resource which, since it is polluting and contributing to climate change, should have been conserved for the vital service it could have performed, and still could, for the benefit of all people. Instead, we Americans have burned it in gas-guzzling automobiles or to raise the temperature in our homes a few degrees. Moreover, as Tom Bender pointed out, "appropriate technology reminds us that before we choose our tools and technologies we must choose our dreams and values, for some technologies serve them while others make them unobtainable." (22) The literature of appropriate technology provides evidence that not all technology has increased the sum of human happiness or well-being. Much "labor saving" technology has been labor-replacing and thus led to unemployment. Agricultural technology has, with the help of energy-intensive machinery, been so "efficient" that millions of farmers have had to leave the farm. And the agricultural environment has suffered more under industrial modes of production than under pre-industrial methods. Much of the work provided by industrial technology in factories, and also in offices, has been on the assembly line, boring and unfulfilling.

The second general observation is that an emphasis on appropriate technology does not imply that all forms of industrial technology are to be abolished. Just as the partisans of vernacular activities postulated a synergy between commodities and vernacular activities, so it is possible, at least in the near future, to imagine and affirm a world shaped by different levels of technology. This becomes clearer as we consider some of the criteria for identifying what level of technology is appropriate. Here is a preliminary list.

— low or moderate capital investment per job—an emphasis in Schumacher's "intermediate" technology which was designed for developing countries. (23)
— local control and self-reliance instead of distant centralized control.
— energy-efficient and sustainable use of renewable energy which is environmentally benign.
— labor-intensive rather than energy-intensive work so as to provide jobs.
— technology that provides convivial and humane working conditions.

— proper balance between hand powered tools and fossil fuel powered machines.

— technology that facilitates equity and global justice.

A list like this, which could be extended, may raise as many questions as it answers. What about chain saws, which those of us who cut our own firewood may prefer because they are efficient and allow time for more interesting and worthwhile activities? What about computers, which have made telecommuting possible, so that people can do paid jobs at home rather than in an office? Computers, and other calculating devices, can do a lot of record-keeping and accounting tasks which were tedious for office workers, but they also replace jobs. Several years ago, my wife Barbara and I attended a couple of Neo-Ludditite conferences sponsored by the editors of *Plain Magazine*. The Ludditites were 19th century rebels against labor-displacing technological innovations and expressed their frustration by wrecking looms used to make cloth. At these conferences we were challenged by the critiques made of various technologies, including especially computers.

Another example of industrial technology is a product that I have always appreciated: stainless steel utensils, because they are so easy to clean and so durable. Again, in spite of the fact that medical technology is much too costly, who among us is ready to renounce it? On the other hand, as Ivan Illich has argued, with impeccable and exhaustive documentation in *Medical Nemesis*, the modern health care industry has generated iatrogenetic counterproductivity as it produces illness caused by medical treatment. Much of this, we can also assume, is caused by the desire for profit by the medical industry as a whole, and nowhere is this as obscenely obvious as in the pharmaceutical industry as it clutters our consciousness with its advertising of dubious products with side-effects.

In conclusion, however, we can recognize some examples which illustrate appropriate technology in a much less ambivalent manner. In the area of transportation, buses for mass transit of people and trains for moving people and freight, should probably replace private cars and commercial trucks. If we begin soon on such energy-conserving options, we could enjoy mass transit for many years in the future. Our dwellings should certainly be designed for passive solar heat, with most windows to the south. "Insulating superwindows in all U.S. buildings could save twice as much energy as the nation now gets from Alaskan oil" (24). Heating water with solar panels is an easy retrofit in most any house. Compact flourescent lightbulbs, and LED lights, use one third or less energy to provide the same amount of light In many areas of the country firewood for heating and cooking could replace fossil fuels and masonry stoves are exceptionally efficient and non-polluting. Such technology for home heating has been available for a long time. (A short article about our off-the-grid solar house can be found at *www.michiganlandtrust.org.*) An appropriate technology for food production, which will be discussed later, is also available. A knowledge-intensive integrated pest management strategy can replace the energy-intensive use of chemicals. Above all, in most of these cases, we need to be aware that progress toward appropriate technology is hindered by vested interests who make money with industrial modes of production as long as cheap oil is available. Thus local control may be not only one of the most important criteria for appropriate technology, but a prerequisite for it. A book which systematically explains feasible alternatives to industrial technology in every aspect of life, from birth to medicine and healing and to death, is *The Little Green Book* by John Lobell.

From Enclosure to Liberation of the Commons.

The enclosure of the commons was reviewed in the previous chapter in connection with the rise of the market economy. In the process, as Karl Polanyi pointed out, land and labor, along with capital, were transformed into commodities. And by land and labor he meant "the human beings themselves of which every society consists and the natural surroundings in which it exists. To include them in the market mechanism means to subordinate the substance of society itself to the laws of the market." (25) If this sounds insane, it is, along with other aspects of a commercial society. And it is absolutely necessary to break the grip of the market economy on our lives as we move into a post-petroleum future. Our focus in this section is on the liberation of land as a commons. As for labor, incidently, it was devalued at the outset of the industrial era, cheapened by the emergence of fossil fuels, as it has been since. In a post-petroleum future labor will once again have a competitive advantage relative to oil.

The reason why land is so important is that it is necessary for the production of food. Perhaps even more important, as agrarian thinkers such as Wendell Berry have argued, is that "land is a gift of immeasurable value" that connects us to food as an organic process rather than as an industrial commodity. Agrarians emphasize the culture in agriculture. (26) As oil costs more our global food system will change. First, it will no longer be economical to transport food from where some of it is currently produced in other countries. Eventually it will no longer be economical to transport food for long distances in this country, as it is now shipped from California, for example. Second, because the industrial mode of farming and food production is extremely energy-intensive, (roughly 11 calories of energy is invested to produce 1 calory of food) the food it produces may no longer be affordable by many people. There are energy-conserving alternatives in organic gardening and organic small-scale farming, and these alternatives, which have been growing at a rate of 20% per year, will continue to grow. Affordable food can be produced, at least in the United States, even as oil costs more. We do not, however, know what the effects of climate change will be, and eventually this will also impact on food production as more severe storms already have. And if more drought and global warming will be effects of climate change, it may be that water for irrigation will also be needed in many areas.

Before turning to land, there is at least one other, more recent, form of enclosure to consider: the enclosure of genes in biotechnology and of the land used to raise genetically-modified crops. While this kind of enclosure is still in the ascendency, its long-term prospects are in doubt. It is not a fool-proof technology and Murphy's Law has not yet been repealed: if something can go wrong, it will. A large-scale disaster would discredit the industry. Because it is a profitable industry its commercial application by corporations like Monsanto, aided by the land grant universities, has expanded prematurely and much to widely across the farm states. If there are adverse consequences, they could be enormous. Finally, because it has not changed the structure of agriculture it remains an energy-intensive mode of production and will not thrive when oil is very expensive. In short, agricultural biotechnology is not likely to survive high energy prices any more than other forms of energy-intensive agriculture.

We can assume there will be strong incentives for people to want to move back to the land. The environmental writer, David Orr points out the obvious: "without cheap energy cities could not have sprawled as they now do, nor could they have been provisioned beyond a certain scale, considerably smaller than our 100 largest cities." (27) Orr goes on to discuss factors that will pressure a new back-to-the-land movement, one, he hopes, that will be well-planned so that people can move to rural areas as homecomers rather than refugees from the city. The most decisive of these factors is, of course, the rising cost of oil. On an ecological level there will be a need for a dispersed population as our society shifts from concentrated fossil energy sources to the dispersed solar energy source. As in the past, meanwhile, there is much that can be done to raise more food in empty lots in cities and on the urban fringe. But a countryside that had been depopulated with the industrialization of agriculture, offers the most hope for new villages focused on food production and local processing in the future, along with space for people to live. Because of cultural inertia, this process of rural depopulation continues. Some people, however, are already organizing into "eco-villages" for the group purchase of land, a process that can ensure both food and community. Mass transit, already mentioned, would have to be part of this picture.

How can land be made available to new waves of homesteaders and small-scale farmers? To begin with, American citizens should be buying land, buying back America. Some people object to the process of development in which larger tracts of land are divided into smaller tracts, but I think this might be in our long term interest. As more people own land less is available for corporations;

we will not want to be serfs on the corporate farm after the end of oil. Those large farms that remain, dependent on fossil-fueled mechanization, are at a competitive disadvantage and they will want to sell or lease land to more smaller farmers. Perhaps there should be policies that require arable land to be used for raising food, so that large farmers who cannot afford costly fuels would have to sell to smaller farmers. For a time, of course, the large farms may try to raise their own bio-fuels. Heinberg points out that the average canola crop in the United States can yield 145 gallons of canola oil per acre of which less than 9 gallons per acre need be used on the average farm operation. (28) But, if manure has to be substituted for ammonium nitrate, draft animals may be preferable. And on farms with livestock, bio-digesters can be set up to produce methane. Eventually, however, it may be necessary, as Orr suggests, that there be a deliberate policy, designed by non-profit neo-agrarian organizations, or all three, to re-ruralize America. Such a policy might make land available at reasonable prices or low-interest loans, or even as a commons, to people who are willing to raise food. Brian Donahue has initiated such a recovery of the commons on public lands in New England. (29) If land is not made legally available there could be widespread "squatting" on land owned by absentee landlords, especially if a local government is too weakened to assert control. Churches, cooperatives, land trusts, and other kinds of non-profit organizations would also have important roles to play in this transition. And, given that much land is owned by large holders, there may be neo-feudal possibilities as well. Remember that laborers will be re-empowered as a source of useful energy and may have a strong bargaining position. Although labor unions are currently in a weak position, they are now part of our heritage, and collective bargaining may strengthen the role of workers in ways that differ from the feudal situation three or four centuries ago.

There could be some salutary changes with ecological benefits in the structure of agriculture. During the industrial era farms became increasingly specialized for mass production and centralized marketing. Cheap transportation allowed for the separation of crops from livestock and for the production and shipping of fertilizer. Manure was, and still is, often a polluting waste product—some twenty billion tons of it is wasted each year in feedlots. (30) In a future of expensive energy, farms would once again be diversified, including both crops and livestock, so that manure would be available for fertilizer and draft animals for power. Amish farmers already demonstrate this possibility. As chemicals for pest control become expensive, (they are based on petroleum) more biological pest control strategies would be practiced. Farms that are more diversified would preserve biological diversity.

This mplies that people would continue to eat meat and livestock products such as eggs and milk. In a neo-agrarian society without cheap oil, this would certainly be possible and may even be necessary since animals can harvest food in areas unfit for cultivation. And it is, as Starhawk has reminded us, the ultimate way through which we are reintegrated with nature. "To eat, then, was not just to take in a set of chemical nutrients. It was to be in profound relationship with a place—with the energies, elements, climate, and life community of that spot on the earth—to ingest the place and become it." (31) We are what we eat.

From Dominion over Nature to Cooperation with Nature in Food Production.

Is it possible to produce food without any inputs, such as fertilizer, to the local ecosystem? It is indeed if the grower/consumer is willing to move from an anthropocentric to a biocentric orientation and to learn from nature. Of course this assumes that the land is in a temperate biome or region, as in the eastern two-thirds of the United States. In raising this topic of zero-input food production I am not proposing that this should be done, but rather proposing a model at the far limits of possibility. For the time being most food will most likely continue to be raised with some, but far fewer, inputs than a fossil-fueled economy made possible. This extreme model implies also an extreme level of local production and consumption. It is illustrated in a diagram copied from an article by D. A. Crossley, and others. (32)

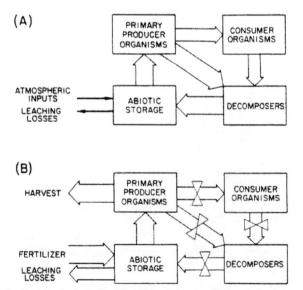

Figure 1. Nutrient circulation through major components of (A) natural ecosystems and (B) agroecosystems. In natural systems internal cycling of nutrients greatly exceeds flowthrough expressed as atmospheric inputs and leaching losses (top). In agroecosystems management techniques include control of consumer organisms with insecticides, control of primary producers with herbicides as well as cultivation and harvest, and control of decomposition through cultivation and plowing. Fertilizer becomes the major nutrient input to the agroecosystem, and harvest constitutes a major output, but leaching losses become larger also.

Students of ecology will recognize the top half of this diagram, (A), as a simple ecosystem. The bottom half, (B), is an extreme version of an agroecosystem, extreme because some consumer organisms and decomposers will usually continue to transform crop wastes to abiotic plant nutrients. In fact, organic growers depend heavily on decomposers to provide plant nutrients and they try to maximize this process by adding extra organic material to the soil. The diagram (B) shows a system in which the soil does little more than prop up the plants—that is, the "primary producer organisms". Heavy fertilizer and pesticide use does result in a simple throughput process rather than the cyclical process implied in diagram (A). But even the organic grower hopes for a harvest and needs to add organic fertilizers to supplement plant nutrients and organically-approved pesticides to protect the crop. For an organic production system we thus need to imagine an agroecosystem which is productive but also uses all the components of a natural ecosystem in which plant nutrients can cycle. We remember that materials cycle while energy (sunlight) flows through an ecosystem.

How can we feel confident that organic systems of food production will prevail after the end of cheap oil? Cheap oil provided easy solutions to pest and fertility management so that strategies of careful ecological management were neglected. Organic methods of crop production reduce the need for fossil fuel by as much as 30%, but they require more knowledge-intensive management. Our situation may be similar to that in Cuba a few years ago. As long as they received oil from the Soviet Union they resisted organic methods. As Richard Heinberg explained, "a small group of agronomists had been advocating ecological agriculture for years previously, with no success; but when oil imports fell and the Cuban economy teetered, the nation's political leaders called on these marginalized ecological agronomists to redesign the country's food system." (33) Clearly, a transition from a global, chemical-intensive to local and organic food systems is necessary as we move into an era of expensive energy.

The success of the Cuban shift to organic agriculture is described in greater detail in a recent book by Dale Allen Pfeiffer, *Eating Fossil Fuels*. What makes this study so useful is that it follows a description of the failure of food production in North Korea after the fall of the Soviet system and its inability to continue providing oil and gas to North Korea. Here is a cautionary tale of how an industrial food system failed during the past ten years after its fossil fuel subsidy was removed. Although geographic factors contributed to North Korea failure, political factors were also of extreme importance, along with the fact that Cuba did not waste its resources on military expenditures as North Korea did.

So how can the ecosystem be productive without external inputs? It can produce food for the humans who plants the seeds as long as the humans live within the system as one of its consumer organisms (returning all waste materials to the soil) and do not use tillage that causes soil erosion. The humans are not outside of the system and do not exercise stewardship or dominion but live as participants in the ecosystem. If all plant nutrients in human wastes are composted by decomposer organisms and returned to the soil the system remains in a closed but balanced state. Thus we can regard this as an extreme case of local production and consumption. If the grower gets additional organic waste materials from his or her neighbors to compost and add to the soil, he or she can enlarge the harvest to provide food for neighbors. But there are limits; if the system goes out of balance as the harvest is greater than the return of waste, the grower will enjoy a short-term economic profit at the cost of long-term ecological loss. In fact this is the case with virtually all commercial agriculture today: the ecosystem is degraded for the sake of profit. Our cheap food policy is possible because, as David Orr pointed out, many ecological costs are "externalized," not included in the price. (34)

The popular literature on organic gardening, homesteading and subsistence farming is vast and will not be reviewed here. But one book that describes the application of ecological principles to raise food and capture solar energy in a closed system (a house on a lot) deserves special mention: *The Integral Urban House* by Helga Olkowski et. al. The fact that this book is out of print may serve as a reminder that we live in an energy-rich exuberant society in which food has been commodified. Even agricultural scientists who specialize in organic agriculture or gardening tend to neglect household food production although backyard gardens produce billions of dollars worth of vegetables and fruits each year—for use rather than for sale. Another massive neglect in America is the so-called "waste of nations," the sewage that contaminates our rivers. (35) Organic wastes should be separated from industrial wastes so the sewage could be returned to the land. The present system would contaminate the land with heavy metals and other industrial wastes that would poison the land. Composting toilets and the reuse of "greywater" for irrigation are a household-level solution to the recycling of waste.

It may sound as though moving from dominion to cooperation with nature means moving away from commercial pursuits, away from making money to vernacular activity. This may be the case, more or less, for some people, but our exercise in ecosystem thinking was intended as an extreme example to help in visualizing a truly sustainable mode of food production. The old book, *Farmers of Forty Centuries,* by F. H. King, described Oriental modes of farming, and they depended on the return of all organic wastes to the land. Where provisions for the recycling of waste are in place, the farmer can raise produce to sell.

There are still other possibilities in ecosystem food production. One is being developed by Wes Jackson at the Land Institute in Kansas: it is the attempt to find and breed food-producing perennials so that energy-intensive and soil-erosive tillage is not necessary. While perennials do not yield as as many pounds of seeds per acre as annuals, some have a net yield of protein that is comparable. My neighbors and I in Michigan have been improving hayfields by seeding legumes such as clover and birdsfoot trefoil on the sod in early spring so that the action of the frosts helps the seeds to sprout without further tillage. Reducing soil erosion is an important end in itself, but there is more. Wes Jackson explained that conventional agriculture has been replacing biological information with fossil fuel energy. When the farmer plows under a prairie, which is a perennial polyculture, and plants grains which are annuals, in a monoculture, he is replacing the genetic material and biological information which kept the prairie productive with fossil fuel inputs to till the soil and protect the plants so that the land can remain productive. (36) It is entirely feasible to recreate a perennial polyculture, especially on a small scale for household use where crops are harvested by hand. In many ways this is what Bill Mollison means with the term "permaculture." An advantage of permaculture is its two-story food production system as it integrates trees with annual crops. Forests can produce food and animal feed, along with many ecological advantages. Permaculture also emphasizes small-scale fish production, an enterprise that will become more important as ocean fisheries are being depleted.

From Centralized Control to Decentralized Local Control

Perhaps the intelligent question here is how much centralized control, and over what, and where in the scheme of things would decentralized local control be better. We now have a system including federal, state, county and township levels of government in most areas. In thinking about social conditions in a post-petroleum future we are not anticipating a sudden breakdown and social chaos. But we are trying to imagine a government that might be appropriate in a time of more expensive oil. Will federal government be as large and bureaucratic? Probably not, but it would be wise to remember that in virtually all periods of human history there has been some central government. Also, less government would thereby also be of less assistance to the people. On a domestic level we may have to do without as many government services, including fewer police services. We can hope that the outward-facing aspect of national governments can be maintained; if they continue to control nuclear weapons we are more likely to survive. State governments might atrophy the most, while county and township officials maintain order and a minimal police presence and generally regain control of various regulatory power that had been usurped by state governments in recent years. The principle of subsidiarity, with control at the lowest effective level rather than at the highest level of government, should come into play and allow for local control and regulation, especially in food production. The age of globalization will be over.

As we consider a loss of centralized control we are in fact considering a partial collapse in society. As one scholar, Joseph Tainter, put it, "collapse is a process of decline in complexity." As he went on to consider the decline in energy availability in our society, he emphasized that "a new energy subsidy is necessary if a declining standard of living and a future global collapse are to be averted." (37) On the basis of his comparative study of societal collapse, Tainter sees difficulties but not necessarily collapse in our future, assuming we find energy sources to replace fossil fuels and the capital to develop the alternatives. These are questionable assumptions. In the meantime, a shift to a neo-agrarian society would be a shift to a less complex society.

So we can expect that, in a time of ecological disruption, there will be a new awareness of the fragility of the ecosystems on the planet which will engender a new respect for the preservation of their integrity, especially in rural areas. Even human interactions could be governed by mutual concern for the preservation of the land. When people understand that subsistence rather than commercial gain for a few is what their environment provides they may learn to be more careful with it. Christian homesteaders may be able to co-exist with neo-pagan homesteaders when both groups realize they care for a common source of subsistence. Even among organic farmers I have seen such differences set aside as growers pursued common interests. This over-riding concern may also mitigate the petty annoyances we now experience occasionally with close neighbors. Accustomed as we are to the commercial mind set, this may be difficult for us to imagine, but the so-called "tragedy of the commons," where people exploit the commons, occurs mainly in a commercial society. In this list of needed changes we are assuming the paradigm shift that will make our survival possible.

As more people move toward living closer to the land they may want to consider reconfiguring political boundaries along more natural or bio-regional lines. Some of this is done already. The river that borders my farm is a boundary rather than the usual fraction of the section. Our township has a similar river boundary which cuts off a corner of the township's 36 square miles. Bioregions, instead of arbitrary geometric boundaries of counties or states might facilitate a keener appreciation of the ecosystem that people live in. There has been a bioregional movement and while it has not altered a lot of political boundaries, it has promoted and celebrated bioregional awareness. Bioregional decentralization might be thought of as the corollary of polytheism, a recognition of the sacred beings native to particular places, while centralized government is the political expression of monotheism. (There are many books on decentralization. *Human Scale* and *Dwellers in the Land: The Bioregional Vision* by Kirkpatrick Sale are good. The most sophisticated is by James Ogilvy: *Many Dimensional Man: Decentralizing Self, Society and The Sacred*).

The bioregional congresses in recent years were one of the sources of the movement toward green politics in this country, and one of the "Ten Key Values" of green politics is decentralization. Having spent five years (1986-1991) working intensively on local, state, and national levels of green politics, I remain very supportive and I am still involved on the local level. Unfortunately, I suspect that the role of green politics will be more appreciated when economic growth is no longer the main driving force in our society. The best the Greens can do until that time is add their voices to the many organizational voices calling for economic sanity and political responsibility. Thus Greens remain a movement as well as a political party.

From Nonrenewable Fossil Fuels to Renewable Sources of Energy.

The primary source of renewable energy is sunlight and it is available through photosynthesis, wind, and photovoltaics along with mirrors to concentrate its heat. Since these sources can generate electricity and provide home heating, fossil fuels should not be burned for these purposes. At this point in time fossil fuels should be used to manufacture the equipment needed for the collection of renewable energy. The remaining oil and gas should be reserved as a feedstock for lubrication, for manufacturing useful and necessary petrochemicals and other useful products. Oil and gas should not be burned in automobiles or trucks or airplanes. For the time being there may be a place for electric vehicles with batteries charged by renewable energy such as wind. Buses and trains can be exempt from this ban. This may sound Draconian, but a national program for rationing fossil fuel should be instituted soon—to extend the supplies and to reduce greenhouse gases. A hefty tax on carbon emissions would also curtail the burning of fossil fuels. The remaining oil and gas will also be needed for the development of whatever technical innovations can be developed to replace fossil fuels, perhaps even hydrogen. A convincing argument, based on economic considerations, for hydrogen as a part of a decentralized energy strategy has been made by Jay Marhoefer. (38) Where possible hydrogen would be produced with renewable sources of energy.

One of the most coherent plans for phasing out nonrenewable sources of energy was articulated by Amory Lovins in 1977 as he contrasted hard and soft energy paths. He emphasized that the soft path would include a diversity of renewable sources that are flexible and relatively low technology. But most importantly he argued that energy sources should be matched to end use needs both in scale and in energy quality. That is, it makes no sense to generate heat to thousands or millions of degrees to use electricity to raise the temperature in a house a few degrees; it is "like cutting butter with a chainsaw." (39) Needless to say, vested economic interests exercised their economic and political power to keep us on the hard energy path. And, as Lovins warned, the two paths are mutually exclusive, especially if the transition to renewables, which is inevitable, is postponed until fossil fuels are so expensive that societies no longer have the capital necessary to finance the transition.

Critique of Lovins' Winning the Oil Endgame

Although I respect his intelligence and enterprise, I have been disappointed in Lovins' current work. In Winning the Oil Endgame he and his staff writers from the Rocky Mountain Institute are proposing that a fleet of light and efficient automobiles could be built that would cut the need for oil in half. The half remaining could, the book proposes, be fueled with biofuels. Thus it is proposed that Americans can continue to enjoy private automobiles, even in a world where many others go hungry as oil becomes expensive It is sad to see Lovins become a shill for the automobile industry, and I think he and his staff are indulging in wishful thinking or uninformed about agricultural sustainability. Without the fertilizers that fossil fuels now provide, even switchgrass cannot be seen as a sustainable crop. And since the crop will essentially be burned, there are no wastes to provide fertility.

Wind is probably the most cost effective and widely available source of electric power and could supply most of the country's electricity. While there are line losses on the electric grid, it is an effective means of even distribution of power from wind. The wind does not blow everywhere all the time. Electricity from wind generators currently costs less than half as much as electricity generated by nuclear power, and it is safer. Moreover, the towers can be reused or recycled. These considerations should have settled the issue, but in 2007 the push for nuclear-generated electricity emerged again, and with support from some environmentalists seeking a way to have electricity without carbon emissions. Money for new nuclear plants was to be made available, at tax-payer expense, thanks to Energy Bill of 2005 promoted and signed by President George Bush. Since the building of nuclear power plants does emit a great deal of carbon and takes several years, it is, at best, a long-term solution. It would have to be preceded by a serious program of energy conservation in the shorter term, a process which could render the nuclear option unnecessary.

For those who can afford it, wind and photovoltaics could provide electricity on the household and community level. Unfortunately, many Americans think wind machines are not nice to look at, especially along bodies of water where they are most efficient. But eventually they will grow accustomed to wind turbines as they are accustomed to power lines. Wind turbines could also be located further from shore. The action of waves can also be harnessed to provide power.

My wife and I have an off-grid electrical system which depends on both photovoltaics and wind since they complement each other. Cloudy weather is often windy. The cost of our system was about as much as many people spend on a new car or pickup. Water is heated with a couple of small flat plate solar collectors and with a loop of pipe in our masonry stove. In many parts of the country firewood is available for home heating, and masonry stoves are extremely efficient. Water heated with renewable energy can be circulated through hydronic tubes in a floor to heat a home. Another, and large, source of heat for the house is passive solar input through windows on the south side. Though it is hard to believe, there are still houses being built that do not even have a south orientation for passive solar heating!

Since the oil and gas used in agriculture and food processing is hidden from view, (even though the average family uses as much in the food they buy as in their car) most people are mainly aware of gasoline, or its shortage, used for driving. And Americans love to drive! The rush to supplement gasoline supplies with the products of photosynthesis, ethanol and biodiesel fuels, while probably well-intentioned, are certainly not a long-term solution. Without the help of oil in agriculture and food processing and transportation, food production will most likely decline or be very expensive. Fewer imports of food would need to be offset with more domestic production. And climate change might also reduce yields of crops. Thus increasingly more land will be needed for food production in this country as oil gets more scarce and expensive. One of the problems with the inequitable distribution of wealth is that the rich can afford to continue driving cars, creating a demand for biofuels which use land and resources needed by the poor. The fact is that the net energy production in the manufacture of biofuels (especially ethanol) is low, or even negative, and without government subsidies they would not be viable. David Pimentel has demonstrated this for several years. (40) Given the demand for corn to produce ethanol, farmers in the United States expect prices for corn in 2007 to be twice as high as they were in 2006. As demand for ethanol limits the export of corn, people dependent on it in other countries will suffer. One type of bio-fuel might be an exception: the production of methane from manure, a process that retains the fertilizer value of the manure. Meanwhile, raising the CAFE (Corporate Average Fuel Efficiency) standards and using hybrid engines with small gasoline and electric motors, would conserve gasoline in the near future. But cars are dysfunctional and should be severely curtailed and replaced with mass transit in the future. As new taxes are needed, a "carbon tax" in place of a tax on income might curtail the use of fuel.

If we are to have energy in our future, it is surely obvious that renewable energy will eventually replace fossil fuels, but the change should have begun when we were warned about energy shortages in the Seventies. The transition process would still continue today, and it would have been done in a deliberate way instead of the frantic rush to supplement conventional oil with ethanol, tar sands, and coal which is increasingly used to generate electricity. The production of liquid fuel from ethanol and tar sands results in much higher carbon emissions so that the United States now generates 33% of the world's carbon dioxide from 25% of its oil. The high likelihood of climate change should have lent urgency to the replacement of all fossil fuels and especially these unconventional liquid fuels. Our political leaders, apparently infected by the mythical mentality of the Religious Right which expects the end of the world, or cynically helping oil interests make more profits, or both, failed to serve the public interest.

As scientists make more information about the amounts and effects of greenhouse gases in the atmosphere available, it is becoming clearer that the most important reason for replacing fossil fuels with renewable sources of energy is to reduce greenhouse gases and thus to mitigate or postpone the likelihood of severe climate change. The burning of fossil fuels is the primary source of the additional carbon dioxide in the atmosphere, but as global temperatures have increased, especially in the polar regions, more ice is melting to gradually raise ocean levels, and serious positive feedback loops are emerging. Some of these are reviewed in a book by Stephan Harding published in 2006. While some effects of global warming, such as more water vapor in the air, are not yet fully understood, other positive feedback loops are already happening with horrendous consequences. If average global temperature increases 2 degrees centigrade as carbon dioxide levels reach around 400 parts per million, sometime in this century, "Gaia could move through a series of irreversible tipping points, such as the melting of the Greenland ice cap, the reconfiguration of the global ocean circulation, the disappearance of the Amazon forest, the emission of methane from permafrost and undersea methane hydrates, and the release of carbon dioxide from soils." (41) These positive feedback loops are far greater than the few negative feedback loops now expected. As a greenhouse gas twenty times more effective than carbon dioxide, methane is the long-term threat, and there is an enormous quantity of it—over ten thousand billion tonnes. "If burnt, methane hydrates would yield more than twice the energy held in all the world's combined reserves of oil, coal and gas." (42) It would be difficult if not impossible to capture this methane for fuel before it is lost in the atmosphere.

At the risk of repetition it is important to emphasize that the first line of defense against global warming is conservation. This is the focus of an excellent article by Robert Socolow and Stephen W. Pacala in the September 2006 issue of *Scientific American*. (This issue includes other great articles on renewable energy.) The article lists 15 ways of decarbonizing energy supplies without requiring changes in our industrial lifestyle. Certainly this will be appealing to many people, like the affluent scientists and engineers who proposed it, who would like to feel that the global warming problem is solved without changing their lifestyle. As Elizabeth Kolbert pointed out, however, the Socolow/Pacala proposals will not be implemented as long as there is no cost to the emission of carbon dioxide. (43) A carbon tax might be in order. And the question of who will pay for the technological fixes was not addressed. The Bush administration argued they could not afford the economic costs of signing on to the Kyoto Protocol. As this administration continues the policies that facilitate the transfer of wealth from the poor to the rich, and give tax breaks to the rich, it is clear that the poor can not pay the costs of carbon mitigation. The topic of lifestyle points to the second possibility: the promotion of simple living through which Americans might find more satisfaction and spiritual meaning. Without some changes to a post-industrial lifestyle the shifts to energy conservation and renewable energy sources will not be adequate.

The fact that China has or will very soon overtake the United States as the world's largest carbon emitter should add urgency to the need for lifestyle changes, here and there, along with technological solutions. Other voices have recently been added to the demand for investments in renewable energy technology, mass transit, and conservation, to replace the energy systems that generate carbon dioxide. These voices include Ted Nordhaus and Michael Shellenberger, who criticized environmentalists who isolate environmental issues apart from the need for jobs and new energy sources. They are not afraid to risk *hubris* in their proposal. "It demands unleashing human power, creating a new economy, and remaking nature as we prepare for the future. And to accomplish all that, the right models come not from raw sewage, acid rain or the ozone hole but instead from the very thing environmentalists have long imagined to be the driver of pollution in the first place: economic development." (44) These are vigorous ideas, and they should be implemented with discretion. Although Nordhaus and Shellenberger do not like talk about limits, their ideas, which require massive investments, may help us all recognize that alternatives to fossil fuels are more costly and will not provide the concentrated energy that oil used to provide. They would, or should, thus lead to more modest energy use and energy-conserving changes in lifestyle and will impose limits.

It would be nice to conclude this chapter with a final section entitled "From Renewable Energy to a Renewed Earth." But, although more renewable energy sources might reduce some kinds of pollution, several considerations caution me not to propose the possibility of a renewed earth, not in our time. First, it is too early in the game to presume that renewable energy strategies will soon replace fossil fuels, given the political power exercised by the fossil fuel and military-industrial industries. Second, the major threat posed by fossil fuels, global warming or climate change, will continue to intensify for several decades, even after carbon emissions are stabilized, because of the lag effect in the massive and complex global system. Third, at this point we have no assurance that the end of fossil fuels will mean the end of the industrial system. If renewable sources of energy are exploited to continue industrial modes of production, the ecological damage will still be severe and the earth will not be renewed.

CHAPTER IV

INTERLUDE: GAZING INTO A CRYSTAL BALL

The word "interlude" literally means a bit of play between two more serious acts of a drama. Any attempt to look into the future should be taken lightly. We simply do not know what to expect. Nor can I use the method of most futurists: making linear extrapolations of current trends, because I expect and hope for a new set of circumstances. But we can play the game of "if such and such is presupposed, then such and such is likely to happen." This is the plan in this chapter. The previous chapter proposed ten changes that are needed as we adapt to the end of oil. In this chapter I hope to express a generalized feeling for the way of life those changes add up to. Some changes on the list will happen under the economic pressures generated by the end of cheap oil, but I emphasize that they are needed. We must accept and affirm and plan deliberately for what is likely to happen anyway. If these things happen in, let's say, ten to twenty years from now, we can imagine what life might be like in around 2040, assuming there is no nuclear destruction and that the possible ravages of climate change are still in the more distant future. There are, of course, other scenarios than the sustainable society I imagine. If many Americans refuse to adapt to the end of cheap oil we can expect the continuation of what we have now: resource wars, growing economic inequity, addiction to consumer goods, and eventually social chaos and widespread suffering and death as the system disintegrates.

Let's review the list of proposed changes that will be needed as oil becomes expensive, and indeed are needed even now, if we are to move to a more ecological and sustainable society. We need (1) a cyclical view of time that is in harmony with the cycles of the seasons and years so that we can forget the illusion of progress, and with cyclical time (2) a more biocentric orientation. We need (3) to move toward a steady-state economics in which (4) the need and desire for money is drastically reduced. We need (5) to be weaned from commodities as we do more and make more for ourselves, dependent on (6) a more appropriate technology. The commons (7) needs to be liberated from corporate control so that (8) people can be free to raise food organically and for local consumption. The trend toward more centralized political control (9) needs to be reversed so there can be more decentralization and local autonomy. And, most importantly, we need (10) to move toward renewable sources of energy and to phase out fossil fuels. This must be done, even if there were still plenty of oil, in order to minimize the damage of climate change. And in each of the topics discussed below, we shall try to imagine how it will be without cheap oil. For most of us most of the time, this means without oil, period. The availability of cheap oil has been the life force in our economy, and without it we can presuppose serious economic recession and a partial collapse of our complex society to a simpler state. As my friend, Kurt Cobb, has pointed out in his blogspot, *www.resourceinsights.blogspot.com,* the average person in this country now enjoys the work of between 100 and 147 energy slaves. Of course rich people with a profligate lifestyle may have thousands of energy slaves, while the poor may have only a few.

Maladaptive Functions of the Market System.

It is no secret that the market system does not always serve everyone equally well. At various times in the past, legislative initiatives have promoted a degree of equity among Americans, but in recent years the balance has shifted in favor of the market system. Or, it might be more accurate to say that as corporations grew in size and power, they took over the government. The market system favors those with more money at the expense of those with less money. A current example of this is the drive for bio-fuels. As prices for gasoline went up politicians tried to do something to reassure Americans that they were concerned about the well-being of citizens. They could have taxed the record windfall profits of oil companies, which were nearly 120 billion in 2006 for the top five publicly traded companies, but they did not. In anticipation, perhaps, of even higher prices for imported oil, there have been mandates and subsidies for bio-fuels. Because ethanol had already been produced in the corn-producing states, it was the most available and easy-to-use bio-fuel.

Although bio-fuels may be a useful transition strategy to ease the way down from the energy-intensive industrial system that we now enjoy, we should be aware that it is only a temporary strategy. Americans love to drive their private automobiles, and this provides an excuse for large corporations such as Archer Daniels Midland, who profit the most from biofuels, to lobby for the production of bio-fuels. Needless to say, making cars that get better gas mileage would also reduce the demand for imported oil, but this very feasible possibility has been a slow starter. The market system is pushed and pulled by different interests, and most of them have nothing to do with solving the problem at hand. It thus works in a blinkered and bumbling manner.

To begin with, we can observe that ethanol is not an alternative to oil, but a derivative from it. Oil is needed for its production, and David Pimentel has argued that "ethanol production is energy inefficient, requiring considerably more energy input than is contained in the ethanol produced." (1) Pimentel included the embodied energy used to make machinery and equipment. Although this negative net energy ratio should have been a disincentive, the fact that it is not is the result of the power of the market system over government. And it is politically feasible because it is home-grown fuel rather than imported. Moreover, farmers (read agribusiness entrepreneurs) like the policy because it has, by increasing demand, doubled the price of corn. So-called bio-diesel, made from soybeans, was a slower starter as a bio-fuel, but has a better energy ratio. It is an alternative to diesel fuel.

There are even more serious problems with this bio-fuel policy. Corn is a food crop, and until it became the main source for bio-fuel, about 20% of the corn was exported for use as food. Thus there will be more hungry people. People in Mexico pay more for tortillas or go hungry. Beyond this is the fact that corn is a crop that demands a lot of nitrogen fertilizer, and this is supplied in the form of anhydrous ammonia which is made from natural gas. Production of natural gas in North America is also near its peak, and while it can be transported in pipelines on this continent, it is difficult and expensive to transport from overseas. Without nitrogen fertilizer, yields per acre would be reduced on food crops and more land would be necessary to produce food. Soon food and bio-fuels are in competition. One would like to imagine that the need for food would take priority, but the market system will favor those who drive at the expense of those who want only to eat because it responds to money. As both oil and natural gas become scarce, neither the private automobile or the industrial food system will remain viable.

Fortunately, there are some serendipitous trends in our society that provide possibilities for the future. There is the vogue for organic food and farming that began as a counter-cultural movement during the energy crisis of the 1970s. Organic farming can provide food with 30% less energy because it does not use commercial fertilizers and pesticides. Consumer demand for organic food continues to grow at a rate of 20% per year, partly because those who buy it recognize that this alternative does not threaten their health with chemicals. By now nearly all organic food is processed and distributed by large food corporations. As a result, advocates of organic food and farming have gradually begun emphasizing local food, distributed in farmer's markets or through community supported agriculture programs. This supports small-scale growers and saves some of the energy used for transportation. Vegetable gardening, even in urban areas, is also growing in popularity. Some people are attracted by eco-villages in rural areas, where communities cooperate in food production. And with encouragement from peak oil groups such as the Post Carbon Institute, with its emphasis on relocalization, more people are moving toward self-reliant ways of life in both rural and urban contexts. If the energy crisis of the 1970s can be seen as a pattern, we will soon see a back-to-the-land movement of new homesteaders in search of their five acres and independence. We will also see more investments in renewable energy and efforts in energy conservation. Nearly all of these serendipitous trends are independent of the market system.

The market system, because it is geared to making money for interest groups, can offer only partial and superficial solutions rather than the needed, and possible, paradigm shift. Because it is maladaptive it will gradually be seen as increasingly irrelevant and obsolete.

Education: Less Schooling and More Learning.

There are some private universities with such vast endowments that they could continue to function long into the future. This is a good thing especially because the knowledge of the past must be conserved and passed on. There is also need for continuing research as society copes with new problems in a post-industrial era. Howard Odum suggested that a course should be offered that shows the relationship of the three "Es": energy, environment and economics. But it is not likely that there will be resources for the many red brick Ph.D. factories that now exist or need for their products. Many of these universities are in financial difficulty already and there will be fewer positions for their graduates. But as long as possible universities should continue to teach students. Like seeds, which can be saved best by planting them out at regular intervals, knowledge must be disseminated.

Secondary education will surely continue but also in a diminished form with less emphasis on college preparation and more apprenticeship programs. Schools will be smaller as school buses will be too expensive to run far, if at all. This applies to primary schools also. In rural areas there may be more home schooling, already a growing movement with its own infrastructure. Assuming renewable electrical energy is available to power computers, there will continue to be a heavy reliance on the internet. The one-room country school may also return. When I was growing up in South Dakota each township of 36 square miles had about six school districts, all within walking distance of the pupils.

When I was a college teacher my colleagues and I used to complain to each other about the very low correlation between teaching and learning. More opportunities for direct, hands-on learning would be of help to students—on all levels of schooling. The late Ivan Illich had argued for this in *Deschooling Society*. At the same time, however, the decline of universal public education will undoubtedly leave more people ignorant. We can hope that potential problems caused by ignorant individuals can be controlled by strong community pressure. In any case, ignorance should not be more of a problem than mal-education by television or the over-acculturation into a consumer society that characterizes so many of today's graduates. I often taught courses in the Honors College of my university and found it more difficult to introduce honors students to critical thinking than ordinary or average students. Honors students were more easily taught in high schools—were more fully acculturated—and usually had more misinformation to unlearn.

Health Care.

The costs of health care are among the most rapidly rising of any industry and the level of care we now enjoy will not be sustainable in the future. Inevitably some people will die if the high level of care is reduced, sooner rather than later. But as my insouciant 90 year old mother-in-law usually comments, relative to this topic, "none of us is getting out of this alive." On the other hand, when cheap oil no longer replaces physical exercise, so there is more walking and bicycling, and if more people actually do physical work, they may be healthier. Also, a society in which industrial activity has been reduced, so that people are less exposed to dangerous chemicals, may reduce the diseases said to be caused by environmental facters, such as cancer.

Since our country, the richest in the world, has chosen not to provide full health care for everyone now, it is not likely that we will have it in the future, especially as the proportion of seniors in the population grows along with its growing need for medical care. Nor is it likely that most of us as citizens will be able to afford insurance for hospitalization, doctors, and medicine. Over forty million do not have it now. Again, since much medical care has unhealthy side-effects, it is not an unmitigated disaster if we have less. Perhaps, instead of the latest high-tech medical care, we need more small clinics in more local areas with nurses and staff for preliminary care, along with more public health facilities to prevent infectious diseases. If pandemics of strains of flu sweep over the world, we can hope for vaccines so that there will be survivors to carry on. But death rates will most likely be higher. As we generally recognize that population must be reduced, it is necessary and likely that contraceptive devices will be freely available.

Media, Entertainment, Community Life.

If the electric grid is still functioning and is powered by wind turbines, electrical appliances will continue to function. If not, people who can afford renewable energy for generating electricity, and there will most likely be some who can, will also be able to afford a telephone and a computer for e-mail and to search the internet. The internet may be an integral part of not only home schooling, but also transmit the regular curriculum from schools to outlying areas. Radio will surely continue to function, but television may be curtailed— first because it requires more expensive power, and second, because people will be buying less of the fewer expensive goods advertised thereon, and without advertising revenue, network television cannot continue. Perhaps there might be more public television from local sources, if there is local funding. In the more distant future we may not have computers or television unless their cases are made of something other than inexpensive plastic, a petroleum product.

Because of the damage television has done to our minds, especially young minds, our society would be much better off without commercial television. For a comprehensive discussion of this topic see *Four Arguments for the Elimination of Television* by a former advertising executive, Jerry Mander. Also, because television has made us a nation of individuals, each glued to our own tube, it has undermined a sense of community. Because people are so dependent on television they may be willing to pay for it without advertising as they do now if they watch public television. But we can assume that money will be scarce. Without television people will enjoy more social forms of entertainment on the neighborhood level. When I was growing up in a rural community during the 1930s, we had, in addition to church activities, a variety of literary and musical societies, band concerts, choral productions, and even a string quartet. It was an intense social and cultural environment. When most food is raised locally in backyard or community gardens, community thrives, as it does when people buy food from their neighbors. A state-wide organization that I initiated in 1991, Michigan Organic Food and Farm Alliance, gave expression to this in its mission statement. "MOFFA promotes the development of food systems that rely on organic methods of food production and that revitalize and sustain local communities." One of the spin-offs from this organization in several areas of the state are community harvest festivals that attract hundreds of people each fall and raise consciousness about local organic food.

If the individualism that television and a commodity-intensive society has generated is somewhat diminished after oil, we can expect that a sense of community will be stronger. In our present competitive society our self-interest out-weighs the interest of community. After the end of oil these interests will converge. As members of a community recognize their common interests, and mutual dependency, sometimes even against a hostile environment, their differences from each other become less important. When I was working in the organic movement, the group that met regularly to discuss common problems in raising food organically was so focused on this topic that it ignored profound political differences between left-wing Democrats and right-wing Republicans or religious differences between liberals and fundamentalists.

Class Struggle: Conflict between Rich and Poor

One of the repeated emphasis in this book has been the disparity of income that has become increasingly extreme. Will the few rich be able to retain their money in a post-industrial future? There could very well be gated communities guarded by Blackwater mercenaries. Given the extremes of wealth and poverty in the United States, it is reasonable to assume that at least some of the more intelligent rich people will figure out ways to preserve their wealth. But even this may not be easy, especially if the society as a whole has moved beyond economic growth and dependence on money. I am assuming this will be the case since I am assuming that an agrarian steady-state society will be in place since the alternative is overshoot and the collapse of orderly society. But will the money of the rich allow them to exercise power over the rest of us? It is not necessary to assume that the rich will continue to lord it over the poor. Oil not only gave us as a society the power to dominate nature, it gave some of us power over the rest of us. After oil the position of workers will be stronger relative to the moneyed class; workers should be able to achieve some measure of independence so they can co-exist with the rich. If the rich hold title to land, however, the poor will probably survive by renting plots of land and thus be in a relationship with the rich. As they pay rent they may be reduced to a level of subsistence similar to that of peasants in many parts of the world today. But if the labor of the poor is recognized as valuable by local governments and gives the new peasant more power relative to the land-owner, the absentee owner may lose prestige and power and maybe even land.

It is also possible that class conflict will erupt between the peasants who raise food and those who are landless and hungry. We can all generate images in our minds, based on futuristic science fiction, of marauding bands of outlaws who pillage the countryside. If people in a neo-agrarian society live in close-knit communities, perhaps in European-style villages with plots of land stretching out beyond the villages, they may be able to defend their holdings. But this implies a Hobbesian world in which people are at war with each other. A more appealing vision of the future of food-producing rural communities was presented by Richard Heinberg in the final chapter of his book *Powerdown* with the image of lifeboat communities. These communities would be preservationist rather than survivalist, preserving and sharing the information, arts and skills of raising and preserving food along with other homesteading knowledge, with visitors whether they be hostile or friendly. Where there is a modicum of local government and order this should be a very feasible strategy, especially if there was also a local governmental clearinghouse which could provide information on where land was available for new settlements.

Rural Life and Urban Trade

In 1979, art critic John Berger published a series of stories about peasant life in France as a way of celebrating a way of life that was then, he felt, on the verge of disappearance as peasants kept moving to urban centers. Berger concluded the book with an "Historical Afterword" in which he discusses some of the salient aspects of peasant attitudes. To begin with, peasants are survivors, not only in the sense that they barely survive because they have to give up the share claimed by the landlord before they can feed themselves, but because they have survived through a difficult history. The attitudes and values of peasants are now more than an antiquarian curiosity; they may have renewed relevance for a future after cheap oil.

First of all, peasants, as they are tied to the soil with no prospects of escape, do not share the ideology of progress that has become so widespread in the modern world. Although a peasant's work may change with the seasons and the weather, it is essentially the same year after year. Thus peasants live in a world of cyclical return. Second, peasants, as they raise their own food, are familiar with vernacular activities. "An intact peasantry," says Berger, "was the only class with an in-built resistance to consumerism." (2) Because long hard experience had taught peasants to distrust innovations that were usually designed for others to make money on their labor, peasants are very conservative. As a result, peasants were of no value to the capitalist economy with its industrialized agriculture and they, along with small farmers generally, suffered policies that were designed to eradicate them.

In recognition of the fact that capitalist productivity has not reduced scarcity in the world, Berger tries to made a vigorous defense of peasant life and values even as he bemoans the fact that peasants are nearly an extinct class, at least in France. But if and when the energy-intensive food system collapses, the pastoral values of the peasantry will once again be relevant. They may even be able to provide food for their neighbors. Or, as they always have, they may first have to produce food for their landlords if a neo-feudal society prevails. In any case, peasants and peasant values have a future. And if that future includes more recent cultural innovations such as labor unions and producer's coops that organize for urban trade, peasants will be of vital importance in the future.

Immigration and International Relations.

During the summer of 2006 the issue of immigration, especially across the border between the United States and Mexico, has become a divisive and highly publicized topic. The October issues of both *Harper's* and *Mother Jones* published lengthy articles on illegal immigration and efforts to control it. Contracts were let for fences along parts of the border with Mexico, along with electronic surveillance. The problem of illegal immigration is divisive in this country because some people, especially those who need labor for industrial agriculture, benefit from cheap labor and the vulnerability of illegal workers. On the other hand, others complain that they take jobs from American workers. Attempts to work out a solution have been debated in Congress.

Part of the problem is created by the fact that Mexico is a poor country which offers few possibilities for a good life, while the United States as a rich country is extremely tempting to impoverished Mexicans. Those who manage to cross the border and find a job are nearly always able to send money back to relatives in Mexico. The effects of NAFTA, the North American Free Trade Agreement, have been especially hard on poor farmers in Mexico.

The issue of immigration will not go away, and it is interesting to notice that it surfaced so emphatically at the time of rising energy prices and as more people are aware that global oil production will soon be peaking. As the climate changes, and as oil becomes more expensive and more labor will be needed, there may be an intensification of fears that American workers will be losing out to illegal immigrants. Given the huge disparities of income between nations, we can expect increased migrations on a global scale as the hard times at the end of the era of cheap oil begin to be felt. This makes me remember a futuristic novel I read some years ago, which portrayed a world of people moving everywhere in search of a place to live. The book, by John Calvin Batchelor, was entitled *The Birth of the People's Republic of Antarctica.*

The pressure of the market will inevitably force people to emigrate from poorer to richer countries. This does not speak to the ethical issue: should Americans, with vast unused acreage, allow immigration to farmers who could raise food for themselves and others, or, as is currently proposed, use those unused acres to raise crops for biofuels so they can continue driving cars. It may be in the interest of the citizens of the United States to allow more immigrants and even provide access to land so they can produce food when the energy-intensive system of food production fails to keep up with demand. Beyond this is the ethical issue of sharing our food or even assistance in producing food, as the philanthropic organization, Heifer Project, tries to do. Sharing food was a topic that emerged after the oil embargo in the 1970s under the rubric of "lifeboat ethics." In one book a group of authors discussed the limits of sharing food with people in other countries at a time when industrial food production will be curtailed by expensive energy. One of the arguments was that feeding people in countries where populations were already beyond their carrying capacity would exacerbate their problems. Garrett Hardin, the hard-headed ecological ethicist who gave us the notion of the "tragedy of the commons," has argued that lifeboat ethics can also deteriorate the value of the commons if it leads to saving lives at the expense of ecological integrity. "To send food only to a country already populated beyond the carrying capacity of its land is to collaborate in the further destruction of the land and the further impoverishment of its people." (3) Hardin does suggest that sending food and energy, if the world were not soon out of oil, might be acceptable. As it is, the long-term shortage of oil continues to make food aid questionable.

In recognition of Hardin's logic, Joseph Fletcher, who promoted a relativistic ethics based on the situation rather than absolute norms, has summarized our dilemma as follows: "To feed and *be* guilty or not to feed and *feel* guilty—that is the question." (4) Needless to say, Hardin and his camp may be too simplistic. Certainly the notion of carrying capacity is complex. We have already seen, in Chapter II above, that the activities of multinational corporations who have grabbed access to land in poor countries, often use it to produce exotic food or flowers for people in richer nations, so the native people in that country are left hungry. The global supermarket has abolished the boundaries that used to separate countries and the spread of the market economy has made food a commodity that people lack when they lack money. Thus it is more than likely that people will move in search of food than that food will be sent to those people unless it profits the "donor" nations to do so, i.e., to dump a surplus. And this brings us back to the issue of immigration. Allowing people to move where land is plentiful, as it is in the United States, rather then sending them food so that they continue to propagate, would mitigate overpopulation there and help with food production here, a win-win solution. The same might be true for Canada and Russia, especially if global warming makes more northern regions habitable. It is likely to happen in any case as we learn from the difficulty of stopping illegal immigration into this country. At the same time there should be fairness. If lack of oil, or high prices, lead to die-off in some countries and reduced populations, the ratio of people per arable acre may be closer to equal around the world.

Current policies of the American Empire are intensifying the hatred many people in the world already feel toward this country. If America continues to expand its military adventurism and risks bankruptcy, we who live in this country may be in a vulnerable position. It is possible, of course, that the end of cheap oil will make it more difficult for nations to wage war. But it is more than likely that military forces in most countries will have access to either oil or biofuels for defense or for an offensive war for the foreseeable future. In the final years of cheap oil, as its peak is imminent, it is likely and only natural that industrial nations dependent on oil will do everything they can to retain access to oil. In fact, this is about where we are at now, with the war in Iraq as the first skirmish. When a country with nuclear weapons is facing mass starvation without oil and has nothing more to lose, they have everything to gain by using force and even nuclear weapons as a threat to get what they need. But after oil, what will a country have in a post-industrial future that other countries will be willing to fight for? In this country we have land, for one thing. But if there are die-offs in poorer and so-called over-populated countries, there may be land available in other countries as well. It is possible to imagine a future when nations are so exhausted that they have no energy for war, but it will not happen until people begin to walk away from the corporations that benefit from trade—and from war.

PART TWO

Religion and Spirituality After Oil

In Part Two of this book the movement is generally from religions or aspects of religion that are not likely to work well for people in the post-petroleum age to what would work better. And since this book deals primarily with the American experience, we will focus primarily on religious traditions in the West, that is, the Judeo-Christian tradition. We shall evaluate aspects of it that are maladaptive and aspects that remains valid and helpful.

Many seeking people today are exploring various movements from other world religions, such as Vedanta from the Hindu tradition, or Sufism from Islam, or Zen or Vipassana meditation from Buddhism, or a deeper appreciation of nature from Taoism. Why should other great religions of the world be ignored in this book? Why should we focus on the Judeo-Christian tradition and the earth-centered pagan traditions that preceded it and the earth-based tradition that are native to this land? The answer is that religion is more than philosophical ideas or meditation techniques; it is a much deeper reality that includes both spiritual and cultural dimensions. As theologian Paul Tillich emphasized, "Religion as ultimate concern is the meaning-giving substance of culture, and culture is the totality of forms in which the basic concern of religion expresses itself. In abbreviation, religion is the substance of culture, culture is the form of religion." (1) There can be no separation or dualism between religion and culture. Our review of the religious dimensions in the culture of exuberance in chapter II can serve as an illustration of this unity.

In many ways this full complex of religion and culture is not easily available to people from another religion/culture complex. In saying this I am not trying to deny that it is of great value to try to learn about other religions. Such knowledge helps us appreciate and recognize that religions have a lot in common; all are human responses to the experience of the sacred even though the specific forms of the sacred will vary from one culture to another. The study of comparative religion helps people to recognize their common humanity in a global world. But when people seek to appropriate another religion as their own they usually end up with superficial or abstract aspects of it, as in the perennial philosophy. Moreover, it has been said that every world religion is complex enough to include within itself all the possibilities that are available in other religions.

Given this emphasis on the strangeness of other great world religions, how can we affirm the importance of earth-based traditions when the Judeo-Christian tradition has always been so opposed to them? In both Jewish and Christian history, this opposition was rooted in the fact that the earth-based or pagan traditions were, as real options for the people, opposed by the leaders of the established religion because so many people found them attractive. They were not strange at all. Many Christian holidays (holy days), for example, are historical commemorations super-imposed on older seasonal celebrations. Easter is one of the most historically-exact events in the Christian calendar, since Jesus was crucified during the reign of Pontius Pilate. But the resurrection of Jesus is celebrated on the second Sunday after the first full moon after the spring equinox, as a seasonal holiday The birthday of Jesus is placed at Yule, the winter solstice, when the sun (Son?) begins to grow in power. The sympathy and kinship many white Americans feel with native American religions may be the result of our "deep" recognition of similarities between native American religions and our pagan past. And, when America is ready to really face the ecological impact of its exuberance, it will, as ecologically-minded Christian theologians already do, turn to the Third Person of the Trinity. This will be explained at the end of Chapter VII.

I have used the words "religion" and "spirituality" without enough concern, perhaps, for the fact that many people affirm that they practice a spirituality but deny that they are religious because religion is said to involve prescientific dogma or doctrines they do not believe. Christianity, with its rituals and collective cultic activities, tradition and doctrinal aspects, is a religion, but individuals within it, such as mystics, may have spiritual experiences. This distinction is emphasized by Sam Harris in his book *The End of Faith*. Writing as a philosopher, he makes a very harsh critique of religions as unprovable systems of doctrine that have often had cruel and immoral effects, but he includes a chapter on meditation and mystical or spiritual experience which he very carefully distinguishes from religion or faith. Another distinction between religion and spirituality is that "spirituality" is often the early phase of a new movement that gradually becomes a religious tradition and may eventually become fossilized. It is on this basis that the sub-title of this book is "Toward an Earth-Centered Spirituality," and the final chapter is called "Recovery of Earth-Based Spirituality." This is an emerging possibility which is being "recovered" from more ancient religious traditions. Finally, my emphasis on spirituality points to a new earth-centered possibility that is opened by a focus on the Third Person of the Trinity, the Holy Spirit. And the image of "Holy Spirit" points to life and vitality in nature as a divine power. That spirit can also be active and creative in each person. This is what Pentecost, the descent of the spirit, means, but it has also been accompanied by the "gift of tongues" and taken Fundamentalist forms. Some neo-Pentecostal leaders have recently begun preaching a "Prosperity Theology" that is uniquely American as it makes the dollar the measure of spiritual blessings. (2) Needless to say, this development moves in a direction quite different from what is meant by the Holy Spirit in this book.

But in other parts of the world, Pentecostal movements are focused on the environment. Harvey Cox reported that in some African countries the Christian Holy Spirit is identified with the "Earthkeeper Spirit" in spiritual movements that carry on indigenous teachings. (3) This is to be expected in places where people are more directly dependent on the earth for their sustenance, and as we approach the end of cheap oil it is more than likely that even Christians in this country will come to understand the Holy Spirit as the Earth Spirit. We shall return to this topic in the final section of Chapter VII.

CHAPTER V

MALADAPTIVE ELEMENTS
IN CHRISTIANITY

As we review aspects of our religious tradition that are or will be less than helpful at the time of the end of oil, it will become clear that this is a summary that includes some issues that were discussed in chapter II. Some of these issues are included here, at the risk of repetition, because it is of value to recognize the comprehensive list of problems in the tradition. This critique may be harsh and uncompromising. In my view, as a person who taught courses on religion in a state university for nearly a quarter of a century, there is nothing sacred about religion as such. It is a collective product of human imagination and thought in response to that which is or had been perceived as sacred. And by the term "sacred," we mean that which has given or gives us the power to live. Since this is perceived differently at different times, we recognize that religions change as they respond to changing circumstances. Much that was appropriate in Jewish and Christian history may no longer be recognized as useful or appropriate today. It is in this sense that some Christian religious thinkers have emphasized the possibility of continuing revelation. As we shall see throughout this chapter and the next, religious visionaries and thinkers respond to this fact of change in different ways. Some seek to revise the tradition so that it can remain relevant. Others call for a more comprehensive reformation, and still others will reject their tradition in favor of more relevant alternatives. In the absence of rules to govern this game, all these strategies are valid.

I know enough about scholarship in religion to expect much disagreement with what will follow in this chapter. Many believers, and perhaps even a few scholars, will totally reject the idea that "the faith once and for all delivered to the saints" should be changed, but it takes a very strong willfulness to fail to see that it has changed. Such people would also probably reject the notion that our energy supply will change, at least until the change is upon us. My hope is that we as a society, or some of us in it, can be thinking about how we can best adapt to reduced energy supplies. If this book stimulates others to think about it too, it will have served its function.

Although this chapter raises questions about specific elements or doctrines in Christianity, it is also the whole religion/culture complex that is problematic. Richard Heinberg has brought this into focus: "As an institution, Christianity eventually became the handmaiden of the capitalist industrial state, supplying the theological justification for colonialism and a work ethic for the factory system. Today, some 'fundamentalists' claiming to represent the true teachings of the Galilean promote an anti-environmental, anti-feminist, anti-gay, pro-corporate, pro-technology agenda utterly opposed to the message of modern-day prophets of social justice and voluntary simplicity. Surely this constitutes one of the bitterest ironies in all of history." (1) A recent book by Biblical scholar Obery M. Hendricks compared the politics of self-professed Christian presidents such as Reagan and George W. Bush with the politics of Jesus and concluded that they had deceived Americans. "What is clear is that Bush and the right-wing religionists and politicians aligned with him have done more to misrepresent the teachings of Jesus in the public square than any leader or any movement in many generations. Along the way they have managed to make more acceptable than ever the elitism, militarism, and imperialism of the Constantinian Christianity that was a a travesty even in its own day." (2)

Some of the most sustained and insightful critiques of Christianity have come from Christian thinkers. David Ray Griffin and John B. Cobb, who have been influential in process theology, have developed sharp critiques of the American way of life and, most recently, of the American Empire. In a recent book they authored along with a couple of other scholars, Cobb brilliantly proposes the phrase "commonwealth of God" as a free translation of what Jesus preached, (*basileia theou*, in Greek), usually translated as the coming of the kingdom of God. He clearly shows that Jesus opposed the injustice imposed by the Roman Empire and relates that to the political context of the empire we live in. Cobb argues that the teachings of Jesus were not only "contra-imperial," but also "contra-religious-establishment." (3) Although Cobb is focused more on the "contra-imperial" dimension, the fact is that it is the unofficial but very real establishment of Christianity as the religion of the West that makes it so difficult for Americans to recognize and affirm the commonwealth of God. Our time, like any manifestation of Constantinian Christianity, is more like a post-Christian time, and only when we see it from this perspective can we move toward an affirmation of the commonwealth of God.

Religious Influences on American Exuberance.

In the second chapter we already discussed how the idea of progress emerged from the notion of sacred history in the Judeo-Christian tradition and how it spawned the culture of exuberance, to use William Catton's phrase. Americans have been profligate, with no consideration for the future since God will provide. Americans like to see themselves as the Chosen People, heirs to ancient Israel, and this is still embodied in our civil religion. Several years ago Robert Bellah proposed a description of the American civil religion: "Behind the civil religion at every point lie Biblical archetypes: Exodus, Chosen People, Promised Land, New Jerusalem, Sacrificial Death and Rebirth. But it is also genuinely American and genuinely new." (4)

The cultural exuberance generated by such images is so deeply rooted in the American experience that it has continued through the twentieth century undeterred by wars and depressions. Bill Devall describes examples of this exuberance in each of the decades of this century. (5) This exuberance can be traced back to the technological aggressiveness of medieval technology described by Lynn White Jr. And it flourished in this country as it was settled by the Puritans who brought the Protestant work ethic with them. This work ethic was described by Max Weber in his famous book, *The Protestant Ethic and the Spirit of Capitalism*, and it is interesting that he quotes Benjamin Franklin to illustrate the spirit of capitalism. Franklin was very shrewd about making money and fairly utilitarian in his attitudes, but he retained the influence of his Calvinist father. While Luther contributed to economics the idea that ordinary secular work could be regarded as a "calling" or religious vocation, Calvin, a more urban reformer, contributed the idea that monetary success could be seen as a sign of God's blessing. Thus the two main reformers provided religious validation to the emphasis on work and to making money as a sign that one was destined to be saved. Weber explained that "in practice this means that God helps those who help themselves. Thus the Calvinist, as it is sometimes put, himself creates his own salvation, or, as would be more correct, the conviction of it." (6) The fact that the drive toward commercial success, so powerful that it drove out other considerations, has these deep religious roots, reminds us that these roots must be cut.

Anthropocentrism, Androcentrism, and Patriarchy.

These terms point to a human-centered, man-centered, and man-dominated world, and because they are associated with the identification of woman with earth they have created a culture that has damaged both. Christian theists are among the most offensive men in this respect, perhaps because they see themselves in the light of monotheism as it opposed the polytheistic earth gods and goddesses. Theologian Gordon Kaufman explained that as Biblical religion developed in the context of a struggle between Israel and Canaan, between the personal moral will of Yahweh and the natural power and process of Canaanite deities, Biblical religion lost sight of its embeddedness in the natural order. Thus the Judeo-Christian notion of God is ecologically dysfunctional. (7) As males relate to a male deity who transcends nature and is seldom immanent in it, so they find a model for their own separation from nature, since they were, according to the story, created in the image of God. In this context the Christian emphasis on stewardship is also flawed to the extent that it is anthropocentric and to the extent that it is like the management of land for an absentee landlord.

In one strand of the creation account in the Bible, the creation of humankind occurs as "male and female". In another strand of the creation stories God created the man first and the woman later, as an afterthought, out of the man's rib, after the animals were created. (What a put-down!) The liberation theologian, Leonardo Boff, lists several items in this complex of anti-ecological elements: patriarchy, monotheism, anthropocentrism and dominion over nature, the tribal ideology of election as the Chosen People, and original sin and the fall of nature. (8). While it is possible to find other emphases in the Biblical tradition which soften the harshness of these anti-earth and anti-woman tenets, they remain most decisively dominant, and they have contributed to the dominant genes in our cultural organism. But they have no place in a Christianity that should help people relate to ecology and the constraints imposed by limits to energy. Ecofeminist theological thinkers such as Rosemary Ruether have taken the initiative in developing the critique of patriarchal domination and in exposing the damage it has done. Ruether's version of this is more nuanced and balanced than most, especially in *Gaia and God: An Ecofeminist Theology of Earth Healing*.

The Dangers of Confusing Myth and Science

We can anticipate a few of the problematic details of this confusion that will be discussed further at the beginning of the next chapter. It will be emphasized there that belief in the myth of the end of the world represents a regression to mythical thinking, and that this makes it difficult for the believer to see reality clearly or provides only a short-term view of reality. Thus Thom Hartmann suggested that members of the Reagan administration worked with the idea that "the world is going to end anyway, so grab what you can now." (9) The preservation of the earth was not considered a high priority. This pattern seems to be repeated in the administration of George W. Bush, a self-professed born-again Christian, especially in his attempts to deny and repress scientific data that conflicts with his beliefs. This process has recently been reviewed by Michael Specter who asserted that "from the start of his first term, George W.

Bush seems to have been guided more by faith and ideology than by data in resolving scientific questions." (10) Specter provides many examples of where the administration has tried to restrict free and open scientific inquiry, such as the attempt to muzzle climate scientist James Hansen when he affirmed the need to reduce greenhouse gases, the American refusal to join the Kyoto Protocol on climate change, the refusal to allow embryonic stem cell research, distortion of data on the use of condoms to prevent AIDS, and obstacles to the teaching of evolution. The cumulative result of these policies has contributed to the weakening of the prestige of science in our society and discouraged students from careers in science. This is a detriment to the kind of ingenuity that will be needed after peak oil when wide-ranging adaptations will be necessary.

The religious Right generally wants to believe that this is a Christian country, even though this belief is without support in the Constitution, and toward that end they have been working to erode the traditional separation of church and state. The most complete and careful study of how George Bush's fundamentalism has shaped his political policies can be found in *God Willing?* by David Domke, published in 2004. The subtitle is more descriptive: "Political Fundamentalism in the White House, the 'War on Terror,' and the Echoing Press." Bush, or his advisors, knew how to exploit the (alleged) terrorist activity on September 11, 2001, by using binary opposites to mobilize support for his military agenda. They are evil; we are good, we are doing God's work. Domke shows how the press was compliant in this binary process, especially after Bush emphasized that dissent or disagreement was tantamount to disloyalty.

Like Bush, many on the Right expect the Second Coming of Christ and the whole scenario of End-time activity as imagined in the final book in the Bible, the Revelation to John, and they then try to relate current events to biblical prophecy. This Dispensationalist interpretation of the Bible is actually a fairly recent invention. The evangelical writer, Tony Campolo, traces this back to John Darby who lived in the 19th century, and it was then embodied in a version of the Bible by C. I. Scofield in 1910, the Scofield Reference Bible. (11) Campolo reviews the different dispensations, beginning with Innocence in the Garden of Eden and ending with the Kingdom after Christ's Second Coming. Dispensationalists today claim that we are living in the final stage of church history prior to the Second Coming. This line of thought is given current expression in the *Left Behind* series by Jerry Jenkins and Tim LaHaye. This series of books is, incidently, remarkably similar to an earlier series of books that my father gave me to read when I was about ten years old. (Of course I am not saying there was plagiarism!) The books I read also portrayed fictionalized scenarios of events that are said to occur before and during the Second Coming. They certainly terrified me! Dispensationalism is opposed by Campolo and other Evangelicals for a variety of reasons: it tends to under-emphasize the church, individualize salvation, ignore social action and support nationalism and war instead, and discount the Sermon on the Mount. As a Dispensationalist, Jerry Falwell was influential in encouraging militaristic action in the Middle East, so this is not an inconsequential issue. Kevin Phillips similarly develops a very strong critique of Dispensationalism because of its Zionist war-mongering. (12) We can also imagine the impending conflict between those who promote a peaceful adaptation to the end of oil and those who, in wishing for the Second Coming, oppose them for interfering with God's Plan for the End of the World.

Others on the Right, especially those in the Reconstructionist movement, have been trying to establish the Kingdom of God on earth now through political power. This would be a "post-milliennial" interpretation of the end-time, in which the Kingdom is to be established prior to the return of Christ. Also called "Dominion" theology, it seeks to bring the country under the dominion of Christ, after which he would return for the thousand-year reign. In many ways this is a more threatening religious movement than the premillenialist option because the kind of religious dominion it proposes, written by the founder of Reconstructionism, Rousas John Rushdoony, is to be based on an 800-page *Institutes of Biblical Law*. Since these laws are very harsh, based on Old Testament models, Reconstructionism is a Christian version of law analogous to Islamic fundamentalism based on Sharia, Islamic law.

One of the activities of Reconstructionism is to provide educational materials for home-schooling, already a growing movement. Under conditions of expensive oil, home schooling is likely to grow enormously, especially among the new homesteaders living on the land. According to letters written to *Countryside, The Magazine of Modern Homesteading* in 2004, home schooling, based on Christian materials, is already very popular among homesteaders. Apart from a political movement such as Reconstructionism, this is a fairly innocuous practice; with its information, it could be vicious.

What we are reviewing here are examples of how our society, under the influence of the religious Right, is being infected with mythical thinking. A mind becomes schizoid and distorted when one compartment in it thinks in mythic images while another tries to operate in the context of science. We see examples of this in the Bush administration where religious ideology trumps science. Kevin Phillips calls this a process of "disenlightenment." (13) Fundamentalism is usually a reactionary response to perceived threats from changes brought about by liberalism or a relativistic adaptation to modernity in a tradition. Matthew Fox has proposed that all fundamentalisms are based on fear. (14) Domke shows that the Bush Administration was very adept at generating and using fear to gain support for its policies, and argues that fear is most subversive of democracy. (15) And the press was happy to promote the fear because it generated interest in the news and more profit. Certainly we are surrounded by fear: in the evening news, which is nearly all bad news, in advertising, where we are made fearful in order to buy products that will abolish fear, and on the streets where we are taught to fear crime. What a change we can see from the era of Franklin Delano Roosevelt who proclaimed "we have nothing to fear but fear itself" to George W. Bush who, to justify his military policies, has sought to cultivate a fear of terrorists and an endless war to defeat them. Although it may not be possible to abolish fear, it would help if there were firm leadership in our society that would preserve the integrity of science and provide a rational understanding of the issues that generate fear. Above all, one would like to think that those who have been "saved" would not be so fearful and anxious about others who are not like them.

Problems With Sin and Salvation.

The stories about creation in the book of Genesis in the Bible are followed by stories about the Fall. These stories are a species of sacred stories called "myths" by historians of religion. More specifically they are cosmogonic myths, stories about the origins of the cosmos and humankind. They are profound and rich in meaning, true in their own cultural context, but they are not scientific accounts of origins, since the scientific method was unknown when those stories evolved as oral traditions. As myths of origin, however, they continue to shape values for people in the Judeo-Christian tradition. One such value is the downgrading of the female, since it was Eve who tempted Adam into disobedience by eating the forbidden fruit and giving him some to eat. Thus this story reflects the patriarchal values of the Hebraic and Mesopotamian societies which generated them. Another problem with these stories is that after the disobedience of Adam and Eve, God cursed the ground so that it would no longer yield food without hard work. Although another part of the story emphasizes that everything that God created was good, the story of the original sin had come to be understood as the Fall of the earth. We already saw above, in the second chapter, that Francis Bacon and many subsequent scientists were motivated to develop and apply science to recover the dominion and perfection of nature that was lost in the Fall. Thus the myth continued to function through the scientific revolution.

It is also interesting to notice that the curses that God placed on the woman (pain in childbirth and subservience to her husband), and on the man (the curse of work), for their original sin, were never lifted by any salvation. In fact, in subsequent stories humankind got worse and worse until God destroyed them (except for Noah and his family) in a great flood. After the flood God gave Noah dominion over other animals once again and even permission to eat their flesh. In other words, the more realistic Old Testament told the story of human sinfulness while the New Testament eventually came to be understood as the story of salvation. By the time that fundamentalism came along, early in the twentieth century, the story of creation had totally lost its spiritual quality as a celebration of the goodness of the earth and had evolved into a pseudo-scientific answer to the question "how did the world begin?" Also, over the years, the doctrines of sin and salvation migrated to the center of Christianity, although they were implicit from the beginning when Christianity emerged as another of many religions of salvation. As this happened the idea of the Fall took on cosmic dimensions, so that people felt they lived in a fallen world, and the idea of salvation was individualized so that people felt they could be saved somehow from that world. Because of the Fall the goodness of creation was forgotten or denied. This kind of Christianity is most prevalent in the various evangelical and fundamentalist kinds of Christianity, and these are the fastest growing groups. And we should remember that this is a uniquely American phenomenon.

Surveys on Religion

Seymour Martin Lipset has reported on surveys of religiosity in America and Europe. "One comparative survey shows 94 percent of Americans expressing faith in God, as compared with 70 percent of Britons and 67 percent of West Germans. In addition, 86 percent of Americans surveyed believe in heaven; 43 percent say they attend church services weekly. The corresponding numbers for British respondents are 54 percent accepting the existence of heaven and only 14 percent indicating they attend church weekly. For West Germans, the numbers are distinctly lower than for Americans, at 43 percent and 21 percent, respectively. remarkable 69 percent of Americans state they believe the Devil exists, as compared to one third of the British, one fifth of the French, 18 percent of West Germans, 12 percent of the Swedes, and 43 percent of the Canadians." (16) I would add to this only the fact that people seldom reflect a deep understanding of their responses, judging from how they live.

It is in the context of American fundamentalism that Matthew Fox has been an advocate of creation-centered spirituality. He gives many reasons why the fall/redemption tradition should be discarded. "Because the fall/redemption tradition considers all nature 'fallen' and does not seek god in nature but inside the individual soul, it is not only silent toward science but hostile to it." (17) This hostility is fraught with tragic implications as it isolates and insulates the true believer from the reality of the natural world. The strength of Fox's emphasis on creation spirituality is evident especially in relation to the ecological crisis, but it is of value in relation to other social problems as well. The prevalent emphasis on sin and salvation as individual experiences not only distracts attention from the goodness of creation, it also distracts attention from the collective dimensions of both sin and salvation. It undermines our sense of community. For example, many Americans who are quick to condemn the Nazi extermination of Jews forget the genocidal practices this country carried out against native Americans. Even today, instead of national repentance and restitution, the trail of broken treaties continues. The sin of enslaving fellow humans and the continuing racism, are ignored or denied by too many white Christian Americans.

Finally, the reliance on a Saviour may provide a false sense of security as we face the severe social problems that will come with the end of oil—or with global warming, whichever comes first. What we will need in this context is creativity and self-reliance, both on individual and community levels. We will need a realistic appraisal of what we humans have done to our earth. It will not help to blame God for our catastrophes or for failing to prevent them. We have inherited a world largely under the control of demonic powers, which, as we saw in Chapter II, are manifest in multi-national corporations that now determine the trajectory of the American Empire. These powers are not mythical beings, but objective structures that grew out of cultural creativity, they have created "symbolic structures that channel human creativity toward destructive activities based on hate or indifference." As these powers have achieved objective reality they actually stand over against the divine power that cherishes the earth and the outcome is, according to Griffin, still undecided. (18) We thus need to grow up and recognize that neither God as Father or God as Saviour are supernatural powers that could somehow save us or the earth. It would be better to follow Nicholas Berdyaev who argued that a religion of creativity should replace a religion of redemption as we enter the age of the Holy Spirit. (19)

This short chapter lists only a few of the aspects of Christianity that would be better forgotten I am not trying to proscribe what Christians should believe, but to make an argument that may help Christians look critically at aspects of their tradition. Nor am I trying to deny the reality of sin or the possibility of salvation. Feminist scholars have been rethinking the notion of sin ever since Valerie Saiving published an article showing that the different experiences of men and women require that they define the notions of sin and redemption differently. (20) A Brazilian ecofeminist theologian, Ivone Gebara, has more recently suggested that "the primal sin lies in the effort to escape from mortality, finitude, and vulnerability." (21) This definition of sin can help us understand the motivations that cause us to seek control over our environment and to trust technology to allay our fears. Moreover, as we have seen in Chapter II, the emergence of the scientific revolution and its trust in technology was a response to the anxiety created by the sense of sin and salvation.

CHAPTER VI

PROBLEMS AND POSSIBILITIES
WITH END-TIME ANXIETY

At this point we must examine one of the religious implications that is intrinsic to the end of oil. It has, in fact, been given expression in some of the books a bout the end of oil. Thus Richard Duncan, in "The Peak of World Oil Production and the Road to Olduvai Gorge," postulates that industrial civilization will disintegrate in 2012 when the electric grid fails and the lights go out. (A brief summary is on a website, *www.dieoff.org.*, along with many other excellent articles about the end of oil.) Other writers, such as James Howard Kunstler in *The Long Emergency*, and, more recently, Matt Savinar in *The End of the Age of Oil*, seem to assume that the end of oil will be sudden and that food will suddenly be unavailable, which, if true, may indeed create chaos in our cities. These are truly apocalyptic scenarios, revelations of the end of civilization. A more gradual process of rising energy prices would encourage people to adapt, and it is this assumption that has shaped my thinking in this book. But even a gradual process will lead to serious problems.

At this time, however, many people still seem to assume that the way of life we have enjoyed during the past century is normal and will continue forever. They apparently fail to recognize that the twentieth century, with its technological marvels made possible by oil, was an anomaly in the context of a longer historical perspective. These people are thus in for a surprise, and they will experience the end of oil as the end of the world. This "end-time-anxiety" is a universal religious structure that recurs in many times and places, especially in the Judeo-Christian tradition with its emphasis on linear time. And, depending on whom it affects, it can have either positive or negative effects. People whose outlook is shaped by supernaturalism, who believe they are "saved" by the supernatural acts of divine beings, (for example, the belief that Christ gave his life to satisfy God's wrath with sinners), such people are also easily caught up in a supernatural myth of the end of the world. It is not far-fetched to suggest that there may be serious conflicts between those who try to adapt to the end of oil in constructive ways, so that a simpler social order can be maintained, and those who look foreward to the end of the world as God's will and accuse those who work for survival as frustrating the will of God.

Premillennialist Apocalyptic Eschatology

These big words, which will be defined in their contexts, point to the negative effects of the end-time anxiety. These have been manifest in people like the man who was President Reagan's Secretary of the Interior, James Watt. It has been alleged, by Tom Hayden, that James Watt told Congress that "my responsibility is to follow the scriptures, which call upon us to occupy the and until Jesus returns. I don't know how many generations we can count on before the Lord returns." (1) Some believers on the Christian Right seem so eager for the second coming of Christ that they may be willing to precipitate an immense global disaster that would destroy the earth.

As we face disasters of apocalyptic proportions, (disasters which do in fact reveal of the possible end of the world, since apocalypse means revelation) including the prospect of climate change as a result of greenhouse gases in the atmosphere, more people will feel deeper levels of anxiety about the end of the world. There will be more interest in eschatology, the doctrine of the last things. A recent magazine article reported on a gathering of "Peak Oilers" and characterized them as the "liberal *Left Behind*." (2) The main concern of people at that conference on peak oil seemed to be on relocalization, or resettlement in a rural area. Although the writer of the article seemed to relativize the movement around the end of oil by portraying it as an apocalyptic sect, he did acknowledge that the end of oil may be imminent. The keynote speaker was Richard Heinberg and his influence was certainly manifest.

In fact there has been a resurgence of prophetic books by premillennialist Christians since 1970 when *The Late Great Planet Earth* by Hal Lindsey was published. (This book, incidentally, was the largest-selling non-fiction book during the 1970s, during which over seven and a half million copies were sold and eventually over eighteen million). Lindsey, assuming the Dispensationalist framework, argues that after the great battle of Armageddon, when the evil world powers will be defeated in Israel, we will see the Second Coming of Christ, followed by the millennium, a thousand-year reign of Christ. After that the old earth will be destroyed and a new earth will be created. We must not fail to notice that this pre-millennialist scenario provides justification not only for terribly destructive wars but for the destruction of the earth itself. It has also been argued that apocalyptic eschatology, this catastrophic view of the end of the world, is a misreading of the Biblical emphasis on eschatological fulfillment in social justice. Theologian Catherine Keller calls for a "deliteralized" and "deapocalypticized" eschatology: "Mary's Magnificat, for instance, proclaiming the eschatological 'year of the Lord's favor,' the 'good news to the poor,' suggests—like all liberation theology, biblical and contemporary—the opening of the sacred community to be realized now, though its fuller realization is still in the future." (3)

Premillennialist visions of the kind described above represent a regression to the kind of mythical thinking that prevents its adherents from developing a realistic, or true, view of life. Grace Halsell, in reporting on her experiences while on a tour to Israel sponsored by Jerry Falwell, spoke to many Christians living in Palestine who were aware of the very different kind of mythological Christianity professed by Jerry Falwell. She quotes a Palestinian Christian: "Falwell prefers not to meet or even see Christians in the Land of Christ because 'we, by our mere presence, interfere with his mythology'." (4) Falwell's Zionist mythology obscured his perception of the reality of Palestine. As James Joyce would have said, Falwell "mythed" the point. Thus we see the emergence of a criterion which can judge one religious orientation that has and very likely would continue to have damaging effects in the post-petroleum era as it justifies the trashing of the earth. Such fundamentalist, or dispensationalist, Christianity, which has grown tremendously during the past thirty years, and is likely to thrive during the hard times as oil begins to cost more than we can afford, must be countered by a more appealing and realistic vision. Very recently Michael Lerner has presented such a vision in his book, *The Left Hand of God: Taking Back our Country from the Religious Right*. His Network of Spiritual Progressives seeks to unite dissenting citizens on the Left into a political force. Unfortunately, the more liberal religious groups have not been growing as fast as the new Religious Right. They have either ignored the Right's war on the environment or done very little to counteract it. During the past few years there have been movements, such as ecofeminism, and creation spirituality, which do challenge the new Right. Charlene Spretnak warned her readers of the Christian Right's "Holy War" against feminism in 1981 when some of its leaders, such as Paul Weyrich, were already bragging that fundamentalists would take over the government. (5)

Meanwhile, the power of prophecy waxes and wanes, waning especially when prophecy fails and the hope it had inspired becomes a more ethereal and vague faith. The flood of prophecy tends to evaporate when prophecy fails, but does not disappear. Scholars such as Catherine Keller have been trying to help us to be understanding of the apocalyptic temper even as we need to reject any literal interpretations. She urges extreme caution in the political arena where the temptation is great to use apocalyptic imagery to justify preemptive military action. She argues that the actions of George W. Bush add up to "messianic imperialism." (6) It is messianic because it seeks to bring the peace of Christ to the world with the power of the United States military empire. And Catherine Keller is right to remind us that we are living in dangerous times, that the world we live in is indeed threatening to us as our collective human actions threaten the integrity of earth and its ecosystems. Although we, as a species, are suffering the result of our own actions, we feel threatened by ecological backlash. Who among us has not felt anxious about the possible end of the world as a human habitation?

But, as was suggested above, there is also a context in which the feeling that the world is ending can have very positive and regenerating cultural effects, effects that can inspire the continuation and improvement of life in this old but renewable world. We turn now to this more positive vision with its possibility of cultural revitalization. And it is crucial to recognize that it is possible only in the context of a cyclical view of time where the end of the old world is followed by the birth of a new earth. The very real danger of linear history, which posits a beginning and an end, is that it obliterates the imagination of a new earth. We have seen this illustrated in the premillenialist mythology of the Religious Right with its emphasis on the absolute End and its acceptance of the destruction of the earth.

Apocalypse and the Transformation of Utopia

Utopian visions have had tremendous influence in Western civilization. Most people who live by the old economic paradigm, those who believe in progress through science and technology, are living in what had been projected as visionary futures in the utopian writings of the seventeenth and eighteenth centuries. In contrast to rude nature, the utopia was pictured as a well-regulated or even regimented city dependent on politics, science and technology. This is the world which we in Western civilization have enjoyed until at least the end of World War Two. At about that time, and earlier, due to the rise of totalitarian regimes, industrial counterproductivity, social injustice, racial discrimination, pollution, and the threat of nuclear power and weapons, we have seen the emergence of dystopian, or anti-utopian, fiction. Many of us have read some of the popular titles in this genre: *1984* by George Orwell, *Brave New World* by Aldous Huxley, or Kurt Vonnegut's first novel, *Player Piano*. This new fiction of disillusionment, along with many science fiction stories, represented the end of utopia. This shift was also manifest in our changing attitudes toward politics and technology which evolved to protect us from nature. Now, as we face not only the peril of nuclear war but the possible devastation of global warming, politics and technology threaten to destroy us, while nature, which had been the adversary, is recognized as the long-lost friend on whom we are dependent.

(7) Advertisers now know they can sell food if it is "natural," without additives or preservatives. This kind of reversal implies also the beginning of a shift on a deep level from the old economic paradigm to the new ecological paradigm.

We can recognize the dystopian sensibility as a transitional phase. In more recent years we have moved on to a second shift in cultural sensibility as the disillusionment of dystopia takes on apocalyptic proportions. Apocalypticism expresses the feeling of people who see themselves between eras, as the old world passes away, usually in some catastrophic manner, and a new earth is emerging. Apocalypticism may be expressed in traditional religious forms, such as the premillennialist Christian expectation of the Second Coming of Christ, (discusses above) or it can take secular forms, such as anxiety over ecological disruption, climate change, nuclear annihilation, or, in the present case, the end of oil. Scholars have recently become attentive to this emergence of cultural anxiety over the possibility of the end of the world through human agency (8)

Apocalyptic visions of a new earth are structured by the myth of Paradise and thus replace or enrich the city of man with images of the primordial garden. Instead of generating speculative schemes of utopia, which are noplace, such visions point to eutopia, a good place, an Arcadian or pastoral scene which is rural rather than urban, natural rather than artificial, and anarchic rather than the product of technocratic management. This Arcadian preference was expressed in the nostalgia for Paradise that was evident in the back-to-the-land movement of the Seventies and in the way in which nature was reinvested with value in the environmental movement. Movements for the promotion of appropriate technology, homesteading, and community economics, along with their books, periodicals, community organizations, and, more recently, websites, have been a presence in America since the Seventies, and they are gaining strength again as we face the end of oil.

Northrop Frye on Utopia and Arcadia

The Arcadia has two ideal characteristics that a utopia hardly if ever has. In the first place, it puts an emphasis on the integration of man with his physical environment. The utopia is a city, and it expresses rather the human ascendancy over nature, the dominion of the environment by abstract and conceptual mental patterns. In the pastoral, man is at peace with nature, which implies that he is also at peace with his own nature, the reasonable and the natural being associated. A pastoral society might become stupid or ignorant, but it could hardly go mad. In the second place, the pastoral, by simplifying human desires, throws more stress on the satisfaction of such desires as remain, especially, of course, sexual desire. (9)

If we follow the thinking of writers such as Richard Heinberg, we can assume that the end of oil will eventually entail the end of industrial food production and a return to local and organic food production. Relocalization is also the main emphasis of organizations such as the Post Carbon Institute. (See www. postcarbon.org). Many more people will be living on the land. Wendell Berry has, for over three decades, given exquisite literary expression to this neo-agrarian way of life in poetry, fiction and essays. It can be seen as an attractive option. Given the progression outlined above, from utopia, to dystopia, to an eutopian Arcadia, we could be on the way toward cultural acceptance of the conditions that will be imposed on us by the end of oil. I have articulated a version of this progression in "The New Homesteading Movement: From Utopia to Eutopia." (10) In this essay on cultural interpretation I tried to demonstrate that the nostalgia for Paradise was alive and well. Even the flight to suburbia can be seen as a debased version of this pastoral ideal. The logic of this progression has also been characteristic of apocalyptic movements on a cross-cultural level. When people feel the old world is dying they expect the birth of a new earth. For example, the early years of the environmental movement in this country began with a focus on pollution, on how the earth has been badly abused and is nearly worn out. But out of this emphasis on the imminent end of the old world, a new earth emerged, and her name was Gaia!

After their defeat the Plains Indians did the Ghost Dance in the course of which individual dancers would go into a trance and have visions of the earth as it was before the white men occupied it. Or, in the last book of the New Testament, as the early Christians were persecuted, John of Patmos was given a revelation of the end of the world along with visions of "new heavens and a new earth," complete with the rivers that flowed through paradise and the tree of life that stood there. Historians of religion, such as Mircea Eliade, have provided many examples of how the end of the world is followed by the expectation of a new beginning. (11) Anthropologists frequently discuss these kinds of phenomena as "revitalization movements," and we shall return to this topic at the end of the book.

If there will be apocalyptic dimensions in the coming energy crisis, as there were in the one during the 1970s, we can expect that they will help to reconcile at least some people to the hard times they suffer as they anticipate "the promise of the coming dark age" after the death of progress. I am quoting the title of a book by L. S. Stavrianos who argued, contrary to the usual view of dark ages, that more expensive energy will bring about a creative upsurge of democratic activity and cultural vitality comparable to that which occurred after the fall of ancient Rome. (12) It is possible for Americans to accept life after oil gracefully, as a chance to start again on a new earth—if they can give up their illusions about progress and the benefits of affluence. With this kind of spiritual orientation it is possible that a future with renewable energy would indeed lead to a renewed earth. In fact there have always been powerful voices in America that have articulated the values of the pastoral way of life. They are a part of what we can call the recessive genes in our cultural organism. Thomas Jefferson has been one of these voices, and according to Leo Marx, Jefferson was more of a pastoral thinker than an agrarian because his advocacy of the family farm was based on values more than on economic considerations. Marx argued that for Jefferson "the goal is sufficiency, not economic growth—a virtual stasis that is the counterpart of the desired psychic balance or peace" (13) Whether the turmoil that may accompany the end of oil will allow for pastoral peace remain to be seen, but it can serve as an attractive possibility.

CHAPTER VII

EARTH-CENTERED EMPHASIS IN RECENT RELIGIOUS THOUGHT

The Emergence of a New Story.

Some years ago I was at a conference, the North American Conference on Christianity and Ecology, where Thomas Berry suggested there should be a thirty year moratorium on reading the Bible. I can still see the look of anxious disbelief on that young Lutheran seminarian's face. But Thomas Berry was not kidding. He argued that the magnitude and diversity of the challenges that the human species was facing required the reinvention of the human on the species level. Unlike most animals, who are given most of their knowledge by instinct, humans gain their identity by means of culture, by means of what they learn. Different cultures have different stories, but virtually none of the older cultures have a story, or sacred myth, that relates the human being to all other human beings and to the earth community. (Native American cultures may be an exception.) One reason for the general lack of human relationship to the larger earth community is that the story of evolution was not available until recently. Thomas Berry explains that "this story, as told in its galactic expansion, its earth formation, its life emergence, and its self-reflexive consciousness, fulfills in our times the mythic accounts of the creation that existed in earlier times." (1) Berry repeatedly affirms the story of evolution as our sacred story, our sacred myth of origin and a record of our participation in this creative process.

Another thinker, who comes out of the tradition of liberation theology, Leonardo Boff, is equally eloquent on the topic of human evolution in the cosmic process. Boff has stayed closer to the Christian tradition and is as concerned about social justice as about ecology, as expressed in the title of one of his books, *Cry of the Earth, Cry of the Poor.*

We do need a more critical awareness of creationism on two levels. The first level refers to the Religious Right which affirms a literal six-day creation in about 4004 BC. Here we see a serious distortion of science which must be questioned. A widespread cultural disregard of science opens the door to the recrudescence of prejudice and superstition, the last things we need if or when there is a disintegration of centralized authority. From the point of view of the believer it has bad effects because it is the manifestation of a schizoid consciousness in which self-alienation leads to alienation from nature. In virtually all intellectual and practical aspects of our lives we live within the horizon of science, and to interject creationism is to distort the sense of reality.

On the second level, all of us in the Western world who are heirs to the Judeo-Christian tradition are creationists even when we understand the myths of creation in Genesis metaphorically or symbolically. The myths of origin, reviewed above, have given us a sense of sin as well as a responsibility to have dominion over creation and care for it. In addition these myths have given us a sense of identity which is difficult to harmonize with our evolutionary heritage of participation in the greater earth community. The older creation myth makes it clear that humans were created in the image of God and, like Him, were above nature and other animals. Berry also mentions the Christian focus on redemption and how it distracts us from creation. Like Matthew Fox, though on a more sophisticated level, Berry is a creation-centered religious thinker. But he calls himself a geologian; his position is biocentric, and does not use, or seek to reinterpret, Christian language. Instead, he and his followers, especially the physicist, Brian Swimme, articulate a new cosmic creation story based on the evolution of the universe and of the humans within it. Brian Swimme's writing is positively rhapsodic, especially *The Hidden Heart of the Cosmos.* As for Berry, a thinker who is rooted in Christianity, he is not just the next step in the tradition of Catholic natural theology, but a quantum leap beyond it.

As he tries to make the new story a universal story on a cross-cultural level, Berry also suggests that the archetypal stories and images (or religious forms) that find expression in every culture—the Great Journey, Death/Rebirth, the Cosmic Tree, The Sacred Center—are needed to provide a deeper resonance to the common experience of humans in relation to the regenerative power of the earth. This is reinforced by Berry's recognition of the "fourfold wisdom:" indigenous wisdom of archaic and native people, the wisdom of women, especially in societies that worshiped the goddess, the wisdom of classical literate cultures, and the wisdom of science as it provides our understanding of the interrelatedness of life on earth. (2) It is this high valuation of archaic and goddess-oriented societies that will be helpful after the magic of technology has failed (assuming it does) and opened humans to life on earth on a level with other creatures. We must also add that Berry's vision of a new earth, along with his harsh critique of the corporate industrialism which is destroying the old earth, betrays a note of apocalyptic urgency in Berry's thinking, a combination of extreme pessimism and extreme optimism. Given the title of his book, *The Great Work*, which originally referred to alchemical transmutation, Berry is surely aware of the magnitude of the change he is proposing.

The sense of apocalyptic urgency is manifest in Brian Swimme as well. In the book mentioned above Swimme discussed the advertising industry which spends over 100 billion dollars per year to keep people busy consuming their goods. He then points out that "the fact that consumerism has become the dominant world faith is largely invisible to us, so it is helpful to understand clearly that to hand our children over to the consumer culture is to place them in the care of the planet's most sophisticated religious preachers." (3) In itself this is an obvious and trite observation, but in the context of Swimme's description of the magnitude and majesty of our cosmic home, in the context of our precarious and incredibly complex evolution, this mode of life where "humans exist to work at jobs, to earn money, to get stuff" is a let-down of terrible proportions. Such a juxtaposition of the immense cosmic environment with the petty commercial culture makes me feel that if the end of oil will also be end our consumer culture it would be a blessing.

I understand Thomas Berry as an earth-centered religious thinker who is reversing a tendency toward secularity in Christian thinkers as he resacralized nature. We remember that Lynn White was quoted to the effect that as Christianity destroyed pagan animism it made the exploitation of nature possible. It was a common practice, as Christianity spread in pagan Europe, for the Christian priests to have the sacred groves chopped down. In the Judeo-Christian tradition it was assumed that although God created the earth, it was not to be considered sacred in any way. It was, however, to be valued because it was God's good creation. As we have seen, the God of the ancient Hebrews was active in their history and was not tied to any sacred place. The Old Testament writers continually chastised the people for their idolatry, for their worship of the local deities in nature. During the past century Protestant theologians have been vociferous in their de-divinization of nature. This general trend was given popular expression by Harvey Cox in his book of 1965, *The Secular City*, as it praised the marvels of technology. (Cox, incidently, quickly moved beyond this anti-religious phase in his thought, to the celebration of religion in *The Feast of Fools*). In any case, Berry was wise to move beyond the Christian tradition in order to resacralize the earth.

Ecofeminism and the Healing of the Earth.

When I was still teaching courses in religion, some 25 to 30 years ago, the only interesting topics in religious studies, I felt, were articulated by feminists who were creating a new approach to religion. I read and resonated with what they were writing then and since then. I liked to think of myself as a feminist, but, needless to say, my wife did not always see me that way.

According to Charlene Spretnak in *Reweaving the World: The Emergence of Ecofeminism*, the term ecofeminism did not come into vogue until the mid-seventies. (4) A major emphasis in this anthology is on healing ourselves; healing the planet. This was also true of an earlier anthology edited by Judith Plant, *Healing the Wounds*. Ecofeminist thinkers and writers do not turn to a mythical saviour to heal the planet. They take it upon themselves to heal the earth that the patriarchal mentality of control has damaged. They challenge the patriarchal notion of power as "power-over" and seek empowerment for all. As women, the "second" sex in patriarchal society, women understand injustice and can, at least sometimes, feel solidarity with other persecuted minorities. They naturally take their cues from ecology: "the interrelatedness of all things in a living, organic universe implies the need for humans to be sensitive to the rest of the natural world in order to maintain its harmony." (5) As they search for models of thinking about the world in pre-christian and pre-industrial contexts, ecofeminists generally avoid both the individualism of Christian salvation and the isolation of the human from the rest of the earth and its communities. Without being overtly religious, they understand that salvation means healing and healing, or health as a dynamic equilibrium, means wholeness, living as members of the earth community. And some ecofeminists, like Rosemary Ruether, who had been on this wave-length since the mid-seventies with her book *New Woman: New Earth*, offer practical details on how to heal the earth. In *Gaia and God: An Ecofeminist Theology of Earth Healing* (1992), she concludes with details on organic food production, local food, land reform, and the need to reduce fossil fuel use.

There are, of course, a variety of ecofeminists, as Carolyn Merchant reminded us in the first chapter of her book *Earthcare*. Most American ecofeminists, however, are part of a commodity-intensive consumer society. Thus the ecological aspects of ecofeminism are a bit abstract, especially as contrasted with the writings of Vandana Shiva. As she writes in the context of Indian society, where millions of people on a subsistence level are directly dependent on the health of ecological systems, she is able to spell out the practical problems posed by patriarchal modes of development as they reduced Nature to a set of raw materials for industrial productivity. Vandana Shiva explains how women in India who work with nature to provide sustenance are producing life rather than money. The relationship of women and nature is more intimate and practical than it is in Western societies. This is reflected in the title of Vandana Shiva's book, *Staying Alive*, and it is summarized repeatedly in this book: "The recovery of the feminine principle is an intellectual and political challenge to maldevelopment as a patriarchal project of domination and destruction, of violence and subjugation, of dispossession and the dispensability of both women and nature." (6)

Ecofeminists have also been critical of what they see as a male tendency to retreat from the possibility of healing the earth in the present to a more abstract, linear, and controlled future. (7) It is certainly true that a focus on the future can distract us from the present. Apocalyptic fundamentalists, who like to correlate current events with Biblical prophecy, also retreat from the present as they predict the end-times. Catherine Keller, already mentioned earlier for her critique of apocalyptic notions of time, proposed that "ending end-time means beginning again with a new full concept of time, a time that has space for us all and a space that has time for us all—a helical time." (8) As we learned from native Americans, the future can be envisioned as a sense of biological continuity, even to the Seventh Generation. This can be more healing and more inclusive than a future conceived in technological wishful thinking or pessimistic apocalyptic anxiety.

It is interesting to notice the inclusiveness of feminist anthologies. They include women who remain in their tradition, for example, Jewish or Christian women; women who have moved outside their tradition, usually toward goddess religion; women who had moved toward neo-pagan or wiccan religion from a secular context, and, of course, secular academic feminists, both male and female. Rosemary Ruether, A Catholic theologian, reflects, in her magisterial *Goddesses and the Divine Feminine*, a broader "small c" catholic inclusiveness also: "I object to any Christian exclusivism and also to any simplistic reversal of Christian exclusivism that sets a prehistoric goddess religion as the true source of feminist faith." She also points out that neo-pagans like Starhawk, who had been Jewish, brought the prophetic concern for social justice to her paganism. She could be considered a Post-Judaic pagan. Or Carol Christ, who moved to paganism after being educated as a Christian theologian, could be considered a Post-Christian in her efforts to reappropriate a "sacred history" of ancient matrifocal religion. (9) This flexible diversity should remind us that a vital religious movement is capable of infinite adaptation and can serve an exemplary function in a time of changing circumstances.

In a more recent book Carol Christ has very clearly articulated the compatibility of feminist and process theology. Her title, *She Who Changes*, celebrates change as the decisive characteristic in process theology, and this title is a direct reference to a song by Starhawk: "She Changes Everything She Touches." Carol Christ's book is a lucid and readable exposition of process philosophy, especially for ecofeminists.

Panentheism and the Analogy of Organism

A philosophical movement called process philosophy, based largely on the thought of Alfred North Whitehead, has had an influence on religious thought that can be helpful in our relationship to the earth. Whitehead also called his a philosophy of organism, and one of his younger associates, Charles Hartshorne, developed many aspects of Whitehead's thought, including the concept of panentheism. In contrast to classical theism, which sees god as transcendent, knowing the world from the outside, as it were, panentheism asserts that god knows and includes the world in his being. In contrast to pantheism, which says that god is the world, totally immanent in the world, panentheism asserts that all is in god but that God is also more than the world. To clarify this Hartshorne has offered the analogy of organism as a way of understanding the relation of god and the world: "the world is god's body, to whose members he has immediate social relations" and "the body of a given mind is that much of the world which the mind immediately knows and controls and suffers . . . but god is that mind which enjoys the fullest intimacy with all things, and therefore in an undiluted sense has all the world for body." (10)

This image or analogy can be seen as a way of trying to make sense of Whitehead's dipolar understanding of god as both primoridial and consequent. The primordial side "of his nature is free, complete, primordial, eternal, actually deficient, and unconscious. The other side originates with physical experience derived from the temporal world, and then acquires integration with the primordial side. It is determined, incomplete, consequent, 'everlasting,' fully actual and conscious." (11) The primordial nature of God can be thought of as transcendent and absolute, while the consequent nature is immanent and relative and can be understood as the Holy Spirit. (12) While some religious thinkers like to pay metaphysical compliments to God by emphasizing his eternal and absolute nature, people who have spiritual or religious experience cherish the relative nature of God as the divine is related to them in the present moment. The same is true of religious traditions; their strength is in their relativity and ability to change with new revelations of the sacred.

If we understand the world as god's body, or as the body of the goddess, we have the confidence that He/She cares for it as we care for our bodies, protecting and healing them. And if we see ourselves as members, or cells, in that body, we care for each other as well. Moreover, if the world is the body of god or goddess, we would not act toward it in ways that damage it. We must bear in mind that these are not just nice figures of speech, but actual descriptions of how goddess/god is manifest in the world. In these ways process philosophy, with its analogy of organism, is congruent with ecology on both theoretical and practical levels. The analogy of organism should be congenial to Christians also because it is the corollary of the Christian image of the church as the body of Christ. Thus Christ and the church are the relevation, in history, of god and the world on a cosmic level.

A few ecological religious thinkers, especially Matthew Fox, in his book *The Coming of the Cosmic Christ*, have proposed extending the image of Christ as Saviour to include cosmic redemptive dimensions. Certainly this would be a way of moving beyond an anthropocentric understanding of salvation. Fox reviews the basis for this extension in the Bible and in tradition, so it is not a total innovation. It opens areas of life that had been repressed in the more ordinary understanding of redemption, such as sexuality or ecology, to Christian affirmation. A much earlier book on this topic by Allen Galloway, *The Cosmic Christ*, similarly shows that the refusal by the Church to move beyond the idea of personal or social understandings of salvation invited the kind of applied science that sought to redeem and perfect a world that was allegedly made imperfect in the Fall. In our time a cosmic understanding of redemption might yet question the worst kind of bio-technology or the engineering of human body parts. In our secular world, however, even this amplified understanding of redemption might not find wide acceptance.

From the Holy Spirit to Earth-Centered Spirituality.

Although Leonardo Boff also affirms a cosmic understanding of Christ as Saviour, he goes beyond this to an emphasis on the Third Person of the Trinity, known in theology, and largely ignored until recently, as the Holy Spirit. This emphasis on the spirit has been impeded in Western Christianity by its insistence that the Holy Spirit proceeds from the Father "and the Son," (*filioque*). The Western Church, always a bit imperialistic, thereby effectively circumscribed the locus of the Spirit in the church of Christ. The Eastern Orthodox tradition allowed for more freedom of spiritual activity, more mysticism, in nature as well as in the historical context, and Western and Eastern Christianity split over this *filioque* controversy. In the West, therefore, the Holy Spirit has been virtually ignored as an independent divine power. And for those Christians who make sin and salvation central in their faith, as many Protestant churches do, the result is, as Paul Tillich put it, "Christocentric Unitarianism." In this context Paul Tillich called for a radical revision of the Trinitarian doctrine so that it might make room for what he called the "Spiritual Presence" which might even be feminine. (13)

Yves Congar, who has written in a conservative Catholic manner about the Holy Spirit, made the *filioque* controversy the main issue in the third volume of his work on the Holy Spirit, discussing it from both Roman and Orthodox points of view. He concluded that "I would say categorically that I am in favor of suppression" of the *filioque* in the creed. (14) This may represent an emerging consensus in Catholic thought and opens the way for the independence of the Holy Spirit in both Orthodox and Roman churches. Yves Congar also cites Church Fathers such as Irenaeus in support of the proposition that the Holy Spirit is active everywhere in the world and among all peoples. (15) The Holy Spirit is truly a cosmic power, not limited to a particular religious tradition.

Just as many cultures have conceptions of a god, so many have perceptions of spirit, and it is frequently associated with wind or breath. In one of his more meditative chapters, Yves Congar observes that "the Spirit is without a face and almost without a name. He is the wind that is not seen, but who makes things move. He is known by his effects." (16) Needless to say, for many recent theological thinkers these masculine pronouns have been replaced by feminine pronouns, and Congar himself provides evidence for this in a section on the femininity of the Holy Spirit. The Spirit is seen in a natural image, as the *ruach* or wind moving over the face of the waters in the Hebraic creation story. The Spirit stirs things up so they do not become stagnant. The Greek equivalent to *ruach* is *pneuma*, from which theologians derive pneumatology, the doctrine of the Holy Spirit, and in more popular usage, pneumatic, as in tires. And in the second chapter of the book of Acts also, the Holy Spirit descended "like the rush of a mighty wind." As religious thinkers today move toward a recognition of ecological issues, nature, or the earth, is increasingly seen as a locus of the Holy Spirit, Lord and Giver of Life. The Spirit is the animating principle in nature. In the last two or three centuries few religious thinkers recognized the significance of natural symbols relative to ecological issues, but earlier, in the twelfth century, Hildegard of Bingen saw the Holy Spirit in nature: "The Holy Spirit is greening power in motion, making all things grow, expand, celebrate." (17) Lynn White's famous proposal of St. Francis as the patron saint of ecologists reminded us of another medieval saint who showed great respect for the spiritual autonomy of all parts of nature.

Leonardo Boff argues that it is the Spirit as conceived in Eastern Christianity, free of the shaping influence of the Son, (and the Church), that provides for the divine presence in the cosmos and in the female. (18) Both a more ecological and a feminist theology require this spiritual grounding in the Third Person in order to avoid subservience to the male-dominated imagery of patriarchy and to develop a "thealogy" (using the feminist neologism) of Mother Earth, or Gaia, as Creative Wisdom. The ecofeminist emphasis on the age-old association of woman and earth, and the exploitation of both by men especially in industrial societies has already been reviewed. Theologian Eleanor Rae draws on this emphasis as she articulates the notion that the Holy Spirit should be gendered as female, and she finds support for this in the figure of Wisdom Woman, or Sophia, in the biblical Wisdom writings. (19)

The Holy Spirit is manifest in Mother Earth and in the feminine side of our nature whether we are male or female. And, obviously, the spirit is the source of inspiration, both on individual and collective levels, and promises the continuing revelation of the sacred. The reality of spirit is transcultural, manifest in animism and known by different names in different cultures. A renewed emphasis on the Third Person can open the way to that which is new and vital on the margins of Christianity as it gives Christians "permission" from within a theological context to move on to an earth-centered spirituality without feeling that they are betraying their Christian faith. It can thus provide continuity within the larger religious community. The Holy Spirit can serve as a bridge to earth-centered spirituality in various manifestations. Christianity is exclusive, while the new circumstances we face require a new spiritual approach, one that can include neo-pagan and native American spirituality.

As a result of the neglect of the Holy Spirit during recent centuries of Christian history, during its period of "Christocentric Unitarianism," there was no countervailing power against the transformation of nature into natural resources. It is therefore not surprising that, as ecological thinkers seek a spiritual basis for their efforts to protect nature, they turn to the pagan imagery of Mother Earth, or Gaia, rather than to the Holy Spirit.

Mark I. Wallace on the Age of the Spirit

"Many people now sense that we live in the 'age of the Spirit,' a time in which a fragile connection with the earth and one another is being felt in friendship with a power anterior to ourselves. The medieval mystic Joachim of Fiore prophesied that humankind has lived through the periods of the Father and the Son and has now entered the age of the Spirit. Karl Barth remarked at the end of his life that the Holy Spirit is the proper focus for a theology that is right for the present situation. And practioners of nature-based religion, from native peoples to modern neopagans, claim that a reverence for the Spirit in all life-forms, from people and animals to trees and watersheds, is the most promising response to the threat of global ecological collapse at the end of the twentieth century." (20)

This is a wise and courageous statement, especially in its vision of continuity between the "age of the spirit" and neopaganism. Rosemary Radford Ruether similarly sees continuity between Christianity and neopaganism or goddess-religion as exemplified by Starhawk and Carol Christ. (21) I do agree with Wallace that such nature spirituality can best be seen from a Christian perspective as a manifestation of the Holy Spirit. Wallace mentions the eco-spirituality that is sometimes explicit in the environmental activism of Earth First!, in contemporary neo-paganism, and especially in the "wilderness pneumatology" of John Muir: "His nature writing is a fusion between a love of God and a lust for the earth that paves the way for a life-centered theology of the Spirit appropriate to our own time." (22)

It is entirely likely that as Christian spirituality evolves under the pressure of environmental concerns it will come into new relationships with areas and issues that had not been considered "Christian." In some places this is already happening. Harvey Cox has reported that in some African Pentecostal movements "a religiously based ecological ethic is appearing," one that "mixes ancient African religious sensibilities with modern environmental awareness."

People are warned to avoid offending the "Earthkeeping Spirit, which is itself the African understanding of the Christian Holy Spirit." Such offences include "activities that lead to soil erosion, fouling the water supply, or chopping down trees without replacing them." (23)

Several years ago, in the context of the energy crisis of the 1970s, Robert Heilbroner wrote a challenging book on the human prospect. He reviewed various kinds of environmental problems, including global thermal pollution, and then argued that the malaise engendered by industrial civilization made it unlikely that the problems would be solved. Yet he did propose one glimmer of hope: "This is our knowledge that some human societies have existed for millennia, and that others can probably exist for future millennia, in a continuous rhythm of birth and coming of age and death, without pressing toward those dangerous ecological limits, or engendering those dangerous social tensions, that threaten present-day 'advanced' societies. In our discovery of 'primitive' cultures, living out their timeless histories, we may have found the single most important object lesson for future man." (24) It is this possibility we must now consider.

CHAPTER VIII

RECOVERY OF EARTH-BASED SPIRITUALITY

This chapter begins with an epigraph from D. H. Lawrence entitled "A Vast Old Religion."

A vast old religion which once swayed the earth lingers in unbroken practice there in New Mexico, older, perhaps, than anything in the world save Australian aboriginal religion. You can feel it, the atmosphere of it, around the pueblos . . .

But never shall I forget watching the dancers, the men with the fox-skin swaying from their buttocks, file out of San Geronimo, and the women with seed rattles following. But never shall I forget the utter absorption of the dance, so quiet, so steadily, timelessly rhythmic, and silent, with the ceaseless down-tread, always to the earth's centre . . . Never shall I forget the deep singing of the men at the drum, swelling and sinking, the deepest sound I have heard in all my life, deeper than thunder, deeper than the sound of the Pacific Ocean . . . the wonderful deep sound of men calling to the unspeakable depths . . .

It was a vast old religion, greater than anything we know: more starkly and nakedly religious. There is no God, no conception of a god. All is god. But it is not the pantheism we are accustomed to, which expresses itself as "God is everywhere, God is in everything." In the oldest religion, everything was alive, not supernaturally but naturally alive. There were only deeper and deeper streams of life, vibrations of life more and more vast. So rocks were alive, but a mountain had a deeper, vaster life than a rock, and it was much harder for a man to bring his spirit, or his energy, into contact with the life of the mountain, and so draw strength from the mountain, as from a great standing well of life, than it was to come into contact with a rock. And he had to put forth a great religious effort.

For the whole life-effort of man was to get his life into direct contact with the elemental life of the cosmos, mountain-life, cloud-life, thunder-life, air-life, earth-life, sun-life. To come into immediate felt contact, and so derive energy, power, and a dark sort of joy. This effort into sheer naked contact, without an intermediary or mediator, is the root meaning of religion, and at the sacred races the runners hurled themselves into a terrible cumulative effort, through the air, to come at last into naked contact with the very life of air, which is the life of the clouds, and so of the rain . . .

It was a vast and pure religion, without idols, or images, even mental ones. It is the oldest religion, a cosmic religion the same for all peoples, not broken up into specific gods or saviours or systems. It is the religion which precedes the god-concept, and it is therefore greater and deeper than any god-religion. (1)

The Loss and Recovery of the Sacred in Nature.

In his book *Patterns in Comparative Religion*, Mircea Eliade sought to describe the structure and morphology of the sacred in a world such as D. H. Lawrence evoked above. The chapter on "Vegetation: Rites and Symbols of Regeneration" is nearly twice as long as others because there were so many examples of the regenerative power in nature. Plants that appear to die and return to life were seen as symbols that express the power of the sacred. For the sacred is essentially power. Religious rites and myths and symbols are religious because they relate us to the power of the sacred and help us participate in that power. The chapter on agriculture, which follows, explains that farming was an important religious rite because now humans were intervening directly in the regenerative power of nature. Although women may have invented agriculture while the men were out hunting, the age-old association of woman, earth, and fertility would naturally have made woman central in agricultural rituals. Thus in peasant societies as late as the nineteenth century, the raising of food required the power of the sacred, and food itself was sacred because it assured the regeneration of life.

During the past three or four centuries the Enlightenment and the Scientific Revolution gradually changed the sacred understanding of agriculture and food. We learned how plants grow. We learned that they need nitrogen, phosphorus, and potassium, along with trace minerals, and we learned how to add these to the soil to make plants grow. If weeds or insects damaged our plants we made pesticides to kill them. We no longer needed to rely on rites to protect our plants or to assure the fertility of the soil. The sense of the organic unity of nature was replaced with a mechanistic understanding. Personal involvement was replaced by scientific technique. Wherever people adopted the world-view of mechanistic science, a sense for the regenerative power of nature was lost. Thus people moved from the sacred to the profane, or, outside of the sacred.

But the worship of power did not simply end. Rather, as people lost a sense for the sacred power in nature they gained a new respect for the power to control nature. The scientist in his white lab coat replaced the priest or shaman as our sacred hero. The fact is, however, that the effort to control nature with scientific technique is illusory; it involved what the ancient Greeks called "*hubris*." This will become clearer to us as we move through the time of the end of oil and climate change. In the Judeo-Christian tradition this effort to control nature is seen as diabolical; it is a form of demonic power as it assumes ultimacy in a power that is not ultimate. We have already reviewed this in connection with the Faustian legend above in Chapter II.

Although modern physics may have moved beyond the older worldview of Newtonian science, that view of the earth is a machine continues to prevail in the practical world of social and economic reality. Carolyn Merchant reviewed the origin of this worldview during the time of the scientific revolution in the seventeenth century, and its results gave her the title of her book, *The Death of Nature*. This is the world we have inherited and, because it was seen as a machine, it has been used and abused since it was thought there was always a technical fix to repair the damage. This is the world that has provided the resources needed for industrial production and the sinks for its pollution. As we have seen, both resources and sinks are nearly exhausted in the support of a population that has now overgrown the earth's carrying capacity. The corporate powers found this growth of human population on the earth to be very profitable, but now that they have almost used up the earth, it is obvious that the paradigm of economic growth has also outgrown its usefulness. Merchant showed that the mechanistic worldview replaced an organic worldview, and in her epilogue she proposes that the science of ecology can help us recover the sense of organic wholeness that the mechanistic worldview destroyed. "The idea of cyclical processes, of the interconnectedness of all things, and the assumption that nature is active and alive are fundamental to the history of human thought. No element of the interlocking cycle can be removed without the collapse of the cycle. The parts themselves take their meaning from the whole." (2) These are the elements we shall seek in an earth religion.

In the previous chapter we have seen that ecological awareness has contributed to the revision of at least some parts of our Judeo-Christian tradition. The theory of evolution has given us a new creation story, articulated by writers like Thomas Berry and Brian Swimme. Whitehead's philosophy of organism, and Hartshorne's analogy of organism, can provide the basis for a religious understanding of the cosmos that is more in harmony with ecology. Ecofeminist thought is more sympathetic to the earth and her healing and feminist theological thinkers have helped in the recovery of the Holy Spirit as animating power in Mother Earth. But most of these are still abstract systems of thought; and while they may help in the development of a new earth-centered spirituality, none of these is yet an integrated religion of the earth which could provide the basic context of belief and ritual conducive to life in the post-petroleum world. Instead of deriving our religion from ecology, we need to identify an integrated earth religion from which ecological concepts can be derived.

What would an earth religion look like? Before we move to a formal description of its elements, it may be useful to remember that many forms of so-called "nature religion" have been part of the American experience and continue to emerge. An excellent survey of this phenomenon can be found in the book by Catherine Albanese, *Nature Religion in America*. She emphasizes, in her conclusion, that "nature religion is just that: religion. Therefore it is embodied and enacted, not simply pondered." (3) A 19th century example of an earth religion was the so-called "transcendentalism" of Emerson, Margaret Fuller, Thoreau and others. Their emphasis was on the spiritual vitality manifest within nature; the tag of "transcendentalism" was given to them by their opponents. They did recognize a divine presence immanent in nature.

A Religion of the Earth

The first important aspect on an earth religion is the recognition of the earth as being alive, animated by a divine presence. It has been called Gaia, the name of the ancient Greek earth goddess, a name adopted by James Lovelock to refer to self-regulating processes on the earth. (See *Gaia: A New Look at Life on Earth* and *The Ages of Gaia*). In terms of Whiteheadean philosophy, it is the world as the body of god, or goddess, and includes the entire universe.

The second important aspect of an earth religion is the story of origins. John Michel, in his effort to help us in the modern world recover the ancient worldview of pre-christian peoples, emphasizes the value of recognizing the original perfection of the world which is subsequently in need of periodical rituals of regeneration. In doing so Michel found it necessary to critique the story of Darwinian evolution. "The traditional view of the life-span of a culture as a process of running down from the time of original inspiration is the opposite of the modern view." (4) The modern view is, of course, the Darwinian notion of evolution as a kind of progress. Michel defends his more ancient worldview as being compatible with entropy, the tendency of energy to be spread out and dissipate. Human history is thus a process of decline which is arrested by human customs and rituals of cyclical regeneration of the cosmos. Michel is proposing a religious worldview similar to that of archaic peoples as described by Mircea Eliade. Thus the world that surrounds us is, in all of its natural features, felt to be real to the extent that it participates in an "extraterrestrial archetype, be it conceived as a plan, as a form, or purely and simply as a 'double' existing on a higher cosmic level." (5) Plato gave philosophical expression to this in his doctrine of preexistent forms and in the myth of a Golden Age prior to civilization.

At this point we have run into a problem. In the previous chapter I extolled the value of Thomas Berry's new story of creation, which is the story of evolution, and now I am proposing that it, or Darwinian evolution, should be replaced with a more ancient story. This apparent contradiction can be resolved if we remember that the earth is the body of god or goddess and as such it also has a primordial and a consequent nature, at least in a metaphorical sense. (See the section on panentheism in the previous chapter). Michel is proposing a view of the primordial nature of the world which is eternal and complete but deficient in actuality. The evolutionary process is the consequent nature of the world, which is temporal, never complete, but fully actual.

It is, incidently, also wise to remember that the process of evolution is not necessarily or correctly understood as a progressive process. It is simply a process of change. Humans have in the modern era been encouraged to think in terms of progress because the idea of progress was already there in the culture, because they loved technological "progress" and because the theory of evolution seemed to reinforce it. Also humans, in our culture of exuberance, apparently felt that our presence on the earth as the dominant animal was the pinnacle of evolutionary progress. As we face a world that may be destroyed as a human habitation through our actions, we may have to revise our inflated estimate of human dominance. Other organisms may replace us as the dominant life form after we have destroyed our habitat.

Michel also emphasizes that the worldview he is proposing includes a steady-state universe and a steady-state society. This is the alternative to the myth of progress which seemed to be supported by Darwinism. Michel proposes Kropotkin's emphasis on mutual aid as an alternative to one of Darwin' emphases, the competitive survival of the fittest. Kropotkin was an anarchist, and the worldview he proposed, and Michel after him, is very close to what we discussed in Chapter VI as an arcadian or pastoral way of life, or as an agrarian steady state society. (6)

Another aspect of this earth religion is that its adherents live in cyclical time and celebrate this process of cyclical return with seasonal celebrations. Most important among these are rites of cosmic regeneration, usually involving an annual repetition of the cosmogonic act, the recreation of the cosmos which was thought to degenerate into chaos during the year. These rites often take the form of New Year's festivals. In this way the past year is abolished, along with the old world, and a new world is born. This implies also a particular kind of anthropology which Eliade summarized as follows: "If we pay no attention to it, time does not exist; furthermore, where it becomes perceptible—because of man's 'sins,' i.e., when man departs from the archetype and falls into duration—time can be annulled." (7) This implies that archaic people found their true being outside of a time that is allowed to accumulate as history. Notice that time as history is not denied, but it is disvalued and time is periodically renewed.

Space is more important than time in the religion of the earth. John Michal illustrates this with the Chinese practice of feng-shui, "the idea that the primeval earth is the paradise, from which, by settlement, we have become alienated; but that this alienation may be mitigated by planning our settled communities and their environments as types of artificial paradise, following the original. Feng-shui provides a code for landscape and building design." (8) In a religious orientation where space predominates it is also likely that polytheism will appear, since special gods will be found in special places.

There is, according to Eliade, another important aspect of an earth religion. In the world of archetypes and repetition, reality is achieved not by the introduction or invention of some new thing, but by imitating or repeating a divine archetype. This is the ultimate expression of a traditional society: a person becomes real by ceasing to be himself or herself and becomes real by repeating the gestures of another, preferably divine, being. Thus Eliade suggested that in a future when humans face their own self-extinction, (a future that may be upon us now) they may want to confine themselves to "repeating prescribed archetypal gestures, and will strive to forget, as meaningless and dangerous, any spontaneous gesture which might entail 'historical' consequences." (9) Thus people might avoid the so-called terror of history that was discussed above. When images and stories of gods and goddesses function as models in people's lives, they serve this function.

We must pause to ask whether these archaic ways can be considered as viable possibilities for us as Americans in the twenty first century. Some Christian theologians, such as Gordon Kaufman, who emphasize "historicity" as a decisive category for Christian thought and existence, argue that the time for this is past. "The possibility is no longer open for us to live a more 'natural,' less historicized, life: human history has moved past the point of no return in this regard." (10) But there are several reasons why this Christian point of view can be challenged. First, these archaic ways are recessive genes in our cultural organism; they are part of our pagan heritage. In his history of ecological ideas, Donald Worster repeatedly emphasized the influence of pagan animism, derived from ancient Greek and Roman writers, and contrasted it to the more dominant imperial attitude toward nature that came with the Scientific Revolution. He saw pagan animism as intrinsic to the emergence of ecological thought, and recognized its re-emergence in James Lovelock's Gaia Hypothesis. (11) Second, we continue to live in cyclical time, sometimes inconsistently along with linear time. Third, we still look back with nostalgia toward the paradise we think we have lost. (12) Fourth, with electronic media our minds are so full of images or models for us to live by that many people have forgotten how to be unique and original individuals. Finally, many other writers are also asking about this possibility. Chellis Glendinning discussed this possibility and concluded that "despite all the contradictions and the myriad problems we face, the potential to know Earth wisdom and to live well upon the Earth lies within every one of us." (13) While she affirms this possibility on a psychological level, I am affirming it as a social and cultural necessity at the time of the end of oil when more people are likely to be living on the land. I do agree with her concluding exhortation that we must "praise Creation," (14) but I would want to go further to argue that we praise Creation by how carefully we use it, for use it we shall.

Just how would a religion of the earth, with its neo-pagan overtones, help us to be reconciled to the earth in the challenging time at the end of oil? As Americans, who have felt we were the new Chosen People, we had enjoyed an exuberant lifestyle with many energy slaves to do our work. How could paganism help us adapt to deprivation? We can find some clues to an answer in the writings of Richard Rubenstein. In his book, *After Auschwitz,* he, as a Jew, questions how God could have allowed the killing of six million of His original Chosen People. As he wrestles with this question Rubenstein is led to reject the Judeo-Christian notion that God's action in history is somehow redemptive. Instead, he contrasts historical religions with nature religions and their more modest contentment with cyclical recurrence in nature with its awareness of limits. Rubenstein recognizes, as the ancient Greeks did, that "only *hubris* is man's real sin, . . . man's sin against his limits." (15) In the course of these reflections, Rubenstein acknowledges the influence of Albert Camus and especially the celebration of neo-paganism in his early writings. As Camus celebrated the joys of the flesh, of youth and beauty, he also recognized that we age and die, and he urged we should accept this gracefully but without hope. "From Pandora's box, where all the ills of humanity swarmed, the Greeks drew out hope after all the others, as the most dreadful of all." (16) Here we see one version of the hard wisdom that can help us adapt to new and difficult circumstances: to live without hope for the recovery of what we have lost but to anticipate the joys of a more modest life on earth—a life that recognizes limits.

From a Christian point of view the ideas expressed in these paragraphs may be seen as a colossal failure of nerve, as a lack of faith in the redemptive action of God in history. But, given the damage done by Christian civilization or Christendom, this refusal of Christian history and its cultural consequences is justified. (As for Christianity, as Gandhi said, it might be a good idea to try it sometime.) A more serious charge could be that this earth religion represents a regression to mythical thinking. In earlier parts of this book we worried about the confusion of myth and science in partisans of the religious right, and now I am proposing a worldview that had been embodied in myth in the hope that it would help us adapt to the end of cheap oil. Also, throughout this book I have been concerned to preserve the integrity of science. John Michal's way out of this dilemma is to contrast the Newtonian myth of the world as a machine with the Platonic myth of the world as a living being. It's all myth, according to him, and he argues that the latter is better than the former. I prefer another way out of this dilemma: the clear recognition that we are *choosing* a myth, and to do so consciously, is to recognize myth as "broken" myth and not as science. It is "broken" insofar as its "believers" know they are no longer "in" the myth as pre-christian people were in archaic societies. Contemporary fundamentalists appear to be half in and half out, and it is this that presents the problem of split consciousness.

The Neo-Pagan Embodiment of Earth Religion

When I began writing this book and told my friends that it would propose earth-centered spirituality, or neo-paganism, as the kind of religious orientation that might be most helpful in a post-petroleum age, many of them expressed anxious feelings about the word "pagan." I tried to reassure them, saying that it is simply a word that means country dweller, and therefore, if more food will be grown locally by more people, after the era of cheap oil, more people will need to relate to country life. But I realize that "pagan" or "neo-pagan" remain highly charged words. Matthew Fox deplored "paganphobia" and he suggests that urban people fear paganism because they have lost touch with nature. (17) Even Margot Adler, who wrote the most comprehensive book about contemporary paganism, *Drawing Down the Moon,* opens with this issue in the first chapter, "Paganism and Prejudice." Obviously the prejudice is ancient and deep—and perhaps even more so in the case of "witch" or "wiccan" or "goddess-worshiper" which many pagans use to describe themselves. It is an ancient prejudice that goes back to the time when the Christian Roman Empire defeated the pagans and imposed Christian rule and religion. Their conversion of the pagans was skin deep, and after the fall of the Roman Empire many of the natives reverted to their traditional pagan ways.

As the neo-pagan movement has grown in our time, it is not as threatened or harassed as it used to be. In my rural community paganism has recently been in the news. Apparently people at a pagan gathering were noisy and upset a farmer's cows (or the farmer himself) and he complained to the township board. The board (or its consultants) drew up a fairly strict ordinance that would regulate large outdoor gatherings. The proposed ordinance was then subject to public discussion for several monthly meetings by standing-room-only crowds. Prior to each meeting the ordinance was watered down to placate the anger of the citizens. Many are simple libertarians who had moved to the country in order to be left alone, but I heard no one use the occasion to put down the pagans. The pagan group was extremely articulate in its defense and other citizens seemed to be willing to live and let live. And the township board gradually realized that it must not discriminate against any religious group—although it did initiate the ordinance because of the pagan group. Eventually the township board failed to pass the ordinance.

The two major writers on neo-paganism in the U.S. are Margot Adler, already mentioned, and Starhawk. Adler mentions (p. vii) that her book was originally published in its first edition on All Hallow's Eve of 1979 in New York and that Starhawk's first major book, *The Spiral Dance,* was published in California on the same day. I read Adler's book years ago and even corresponded with her about it when it came out. But I have to acknowledge that it is Starhawk's most recent book, *The Earth Path: Grounding Your Spirit in the Rhythms of Nature,* that recharged my enthusiasm for neo-paganism, especially in relation to this writing. Another author, who has more recently written books on the end of oil, Richard Heinberg, had earlier written books which called for the celebration of nature in somewhat pagan ways: *Memories and Visions of Paradise,* 1989, *Celebrate the Solstice,* 1993, and *A New Covenant with Nature,* 1996.

We can turn now to pagan writings and writings about paganism as we explore the main aspects of earth religion. The first is the recognition that the earth is alive. Margot Adler, in reviewing the pagan world view, lists animism, pantheism and polytheism as the beliefs that most pagans can agree on. (18) Animism is the view that everything partakes of the life force, and while it is a primitive insight, it has its corollary in modern process philosophy in the doctrine of panpsychism, the notion that everything has feelings. Virtually all mystics also come to this recognition of animism. Other neo-pagans affirm pantheism and polytheism, and more sophisticated goddess worshipers, such as Carol Christ, affirm panentheism, that the world is the body of the goddess. This idea is implicit among neo-pagans also. Polytheism is inevitable in any earth religion that recognizes the land and space more generally as a sacred reality, since every unique bioregion has its deity.

Regardless of how different neo-pagans envision gods and goddesses, these divine images function as their archetypes that embody the original perfection. (19) It is important to keep in mind that neo-pagans do not simply believe in their divine beings; they call them into the circle or evoke them in ritual. Most pagans are supportive of science and technology, especially ecology. Starhawk, a strong partisan of science, articulates a "Gaian evolution" that "becomes the story of how the planet herself comes alive." (20) She explicitly rejects social Darwinism and the possibility that evolution is progress. Neo-pagans are also anarchistic and extremely individualistic. They are usually members of a small coven, especially if they identify as wiccans, but most do not identify with a larger religious community. This may change as neo-paganism evolves into a religious group with national coordination.

Adler repeatedly emphasizes that neo-pagans express a wide diversity of opinion on most any issue. For example, when she questioned people about the idea that the Western linear notion of time, instead of a cyclic notion, has produced a society based on exploitation, she found that "a few Neo-Pagans accepted this view. Many rejected it. Most had never thought about it." (21) Adler emphasizes that neo-pagans are ordinary Americans. She also reports that as a whole the neo-pagan movement has become more informed and sophisticated since she began her study in the mid-seventies, especially as ecofeminism emerged. According to Erik Davis, who has written about "technopagans," a fringe of the more magically-oriented neo-pagans have made themselves more at home in cyberspace than in the countryside. Among these he sees a kind of "technoanimism": "the computer is the most animated and intelligent of machines, the most 'interactive' and by far the least 'mechanical'." (22) Neo-pagans are a very diverse group.

Surely one of the most universal aspects of neo-paganism is its emphasis on cyclical structures. This is manifest in seasonal celebrations, which can celebrate the waxing and waning of the moon, and the wheel of the year which celebrates the cycle of the earth around the sun. Nearly any handbook on witchcraft or pagan practices describes these cycles and the rituals appropriate to celebrate them. In casting a circle to create a sacred space for a ritual it is common to acknowledge the four directions and their powers. Although there are many variations, the power of light and motion may be in the east; the power of fire and energy is in the south; the power of water and flow is in the west; and the power of earth is in the north. All these cyclical images reflect and embody a cyclical sense of time and its eternal return.

But what makes Starhawk's most recent book, *The Earth Path*, so very valuable is the way she relates the cyclical structures to the realities of modern life, thus "grounding your spirit in the rhythms of nature," to quote her subtitle. After a chapter on "The Circle of Life" she has chapters on "Air," "Fire," "Water," and "Earth," the four elements. The chapter on air includes a section on global warming and climate change. The chapter on fire includes sections on the flow of energy in living systems and a description of the simple system of renewable energy in her cabin. The chapter on water, which is often scarce where she lives in California, includes a section on saving and conserving water. The chapter on earth includes sections on the global corporate food system and, of course, on gardening and making compost. And each of these chapters include rituals which often have very practical applications.

As he urged the celebration of the solstice, Richard Heinberg suggested that the harmony between women and men, and humanity and nature, which was lost after the perfection of the Golden Age, could be brought into balance again in the celebration of the solstice. In celebrating the polarities the original harmony is reestablished and the world is renewed. (23) The summer solstice, which celebrates the sun at its greatest power, is especially important for us as we enter the solar age. Traditionally, it was the Earth day which celebrated the divine female. In many such celebrations the winter solstice was the time when the divine male was dominant for his half of the year, and thus there was a balance of gendered power.

A recent book, *Pagan Visions for a Sustainable Future*, written largely by English and Australian pagans, begins and ends with articles on sacred community and sacred relationships generally. The final essay, by one of the editors of the book, Thom van Dooren, is called "Dwelling in Sacred Community," (24) and by "dwelling" he means an active life in a particular place. This includes a relationship to death as we produce and prepare our food, for it is based on killing animals or plants. He argues that the eater needs to do this or be fully aware of the process. Our wastes must be returned to the earth as much as possible so that the cycle of death and life can be complete. Seasonal celebrations become real and meaningful to the extent that the celebrant actually participates in the seasonal cycle of life and death. He argues against factors in modern life that depersonalize our sense of community, and this includes excessive technology, commodification, and global trade.

The neo-pagan movement continues to grow. In the 1986 edition of her study, Adler gives an estimate of 100,000, (25) and the number of neo-pagans has surely grown since then. By way of comparison, Adler points out that there are roughly 180,000 Unitarians and 40,000 Quakers. A British author asserted that among religious movements aside from Christianity, "the fastest growing in the United States is Paganism." He went on to say that modern witches do not "fly on broomsticks, hold sacrifices, worship the Devil, or indulge in orgies. Indeed, it is highly unlikely that witches, the 'wise women' and healers of old, ever did these things." (26) The neo-pagan movement has gained considerable recognition as a legitimate religious body and, in 1987, was accepted as the Covenant of Unitarian Universalist Pagans, a legitimate religious option within the Unitarian Universalist denomination. (27) This group now serves as a sort of clearinghouse for other pagans.

Some neo-pagans have joined with compatible groups in ecology actions and political protests. Starhawk has been exceptionally active in protest and demonstration and had been arrested 14 times by 1986. (28) My wife, Barbara, who had lived in San Francisco for 20 years, was in jail with Starhawk and others a couple of times in the early 1980s when the Livermore Action Group did demonstrations protesting the development of nuclear weapons. She remembers that even in their group confinement Starhawk organized rituals that empowered the women.

Although most neo-pagans, like most Americans, live in cities, many have expressed the wish to live in the country. Some actually make the move. Starhawk divides her time between places in and north of San Francisco and puts great emphasis on fully dwelling on the land versus merely maintaining a rural residence. Many of the practitioners of Wicca who write handbooks on ritual seem to presuppose a country setting. Rhiannon Ryall emphasized that originally all rituals were outdoors: "I an always amazed how city dwellers try to follow the old religion . . . . The Craft is a religion of the earth, and its practitioners were earthy." (29) Adler, herself a partisan of city life, tends to be defensive about people who prefer city life. She does recognize that some neo-pagans affirm that "neo-paganism is the back-to-the-land movement." (30) But she reports that many did not think a massive back-to-the-land movement was appropriate. If the era of expensive oil prompts a process of deurbanization, it is reasonable to assume, or at least to hope, that the neo-pagans will be in the vanguard of those going back to the land.

Gaia and Goddess Spirituality

The image of Gaia, the name of the ancient Greek earth goddess, has come into the current conversation from two sources. On the one hand ecofeminists have reclaimed the image of Gaia as they emphasize the healing of the earth. On the other hand, James Lovelock and Lynn Margulis (with a little help from novelist William Golding) selected the image of Gaia as a personification of the earth as a self-regulating system that is able to adapt to changing conditions and maintain homeostasis. According to more recent reports, however, (See *The Revenge of Gaia*) Lovelock seems to have lost faith in this self-regulating ability as greenhouse gases continue to concentrate in the atmosphere and global temperatures rise and glaciers melt. As I write this, early in 2006, global warming is finally acknowledged in the mainstream press and it is likely, eventually, to be the main incentive for legislation designed to reduce the burning of fossil fuels. If this happens it would be a constructive result insofar as the remaining oil could be used where absolutely necessary, at a radically reduced rate, for a long time to come. Certainly the healing of Mother Earth depends on reducing the rate at which her children burn fossil fuels.

Ecofeminists who affirm Gaia as the earth goddess go beyond Lovelock, who sometimes said he did not intend that his theory should imply that the earth is a living divine being. But he does speak of Gaia as though she were a goddess. "Gaia, as I see her, is no doting mother tolerant of misdemeanors, nor is she some fragile and delicate damsel in danger from brutal mankind. She is stern and tough, always keeping the world warm and comfortable for those who obey the rules, but ruthless in her destruction of those who transgress" (31) If this anthropomorphic language is not meant literally, it certainly sounds as if the Earth is a willful being. Stephan Harding has, in a book just published, sought to rehabilitate the animistic vision of the earth as a living being. Holistic science, he explains, "weaves together the empirical and the archetypal aspects of the mind so that they work together as equal partners in a quest that aims not at a complete understanding and mastery of nature, but rather that strives for genuine participation with nature." (32) A part of this understanding includes the idea of "panpsychism" similar to that expounded by process philosophy. Even matter is sentient. Harding argues that it is through such holistic thinking that we can come to Gaian knowledge of the earth as a living being. I have always felt this way about reality, and thus wrote about demonic structures, and of culture as an organism, but Harding explains how this could be scientifically justified.

Many goddess-worshipers seem quite willing to replace the male god of the Judeo-Christian tradition with the earth mother. Others, like Rosemary Ruether, opened her book, *Gaia and God*, with the question: "Are Gaia, the living and sacred earth, and God, the monotheistic deity of the biblical traditions, on speaking terms with each other"? As Ruether reviews the healing of Gaia she does see some current trends in ecological awareness among Christian thinkers, most of which were mentioned in the previous chapter. If these ecological emphases among Christian thinkers are affirmed, and if Christians cease their anti-pagan diatribes, Ruether sees a future for the Christian God in relation to Gaia. She expresses appreciation for the prophetic emphasis on social justice, and throughout her career she has focused on practical solutions to theoretical problems. "Our model . . . expresses itself in a new command to learn to cultivate the garden, for the cultivation of the garden is where the powers of rational consciousness come together with the harmonies of nature in partnership." (33) This was first published in 1972.

Many Christian feminists who recognize the relevance of goddess talk are in a difficult position as their thinking is still shaped by the Second Person of the Trinity. Thus the free action of the Spirit is always constrained by the maleness of Christ or channeled through the Church. In the previous chapter I have suggested another possibility; a deeper contemporary goddess "thealogy" that could be affirmed as an earth-centered continuation of the tradition in terms of a "thealogy" of the Holy Spirit. Many Christian thinkers have related the Holy Spirit to Wisdom (Sophia) and generally to a feminine presence. (34) Christ and the Church were the fuller revelation of God in history, but they have given us a very dim view of the sacredness of nature and the earth. Many goddess-worshipers today, such as Carol Christ, have found it necessary to separate themselves from the Christian tradition in order to affirm the goddess, and they report that this movement was helped by neo-pagan witches like Z Budapest and Starhawk. (35) Others, like Charlene Spretnak, remain in the Christian tradition, even as they critique its patriarchal bias. Spretnak's recent book, *Missing Mary*, argues for the reclamation of Mary in the Catholic Church as manifestation of the Divine Feminine. She had earlier written about the goddesses of ancient Greece and in *States of Grace* she emphasized goddess rituals for their value as embodiments of the sacred.

This separation from the tradition by some ecofeminist thinkers is fully justified by the fact that as women they could not find their own religious identity in a male dominated tradition with male deities. Carol Christ repeatedly complains about how she had been denigrated and put down by her father, her male professors, and the male deities in Christianity, and she reports finding a more congenial spiritual environment in Greece, where she found the goddess in caves near ancient temples. But she also acknowledges that the experience of living among people in Greece, who live closer to the land, helped her to sense the presence of the goddess. (36) Her life in Greece has also sharpened her awareness of the ecological web of life, though this does not seem as important to her as it is to many other ecofeminist thinkers. Her major contribution is to the development of a thealogy of the goddess. In *Laughter of Aphrodite*, which includes some of her best writing, she expresses veneration for Gaia and Aphrodite, as well as Demeter and Persephone, but goes on to say that "underlying each of these differentiated Goddesses is Earth, the pulsing energy of life, death and rebirth." (37) It will be extremely important to recognize the earth as Mother Earth as we move into an era when the earth is in need of more respect and care, and this is an emphasis common to all earth-based spiritual traditions. To see the Earth as the body of the Goddess should help to generate respect for Her.

There is also a large body of writing that explains and promotes goddess spirituality on more popular and practical levels. It frequently reviews current feminist issues in relation to more ancient lore. Demetra George, for example, relates the well-being of women to the moon, not only in its monthly or annual cycles, but also in its precessional cycles through the signs of the zodiac in a cycle of 26,000 years. In her book, *Mysteries of the Dark Moon*, she explains the disappearance of goddess religion in relation to the dark phase of lunar cycles and not simply to patriarchal repression. (38) She also elucidates, along with many other writers, the archetypal images associated with the dark goddess, such as Lilith, along with the symbols of the snake, the cosmic tree, and the mysteries of birth, death and rebirth. The image of Lilith, who had been, according to rabbinic legend, Adam's first wife, recurs in other feminist writings because she was equal to and not subservient to Adam. (39) And because many people are both goddess-worshipers and neo-pagans, their common concerns overlap as they seek the healing of the earth. Many of these writers understand the importance of the agricultural cycle in relation to larger cosmic cycles. Other more radical feminist religious writers have suggested that the Cross should be replaced by the Cosmic Tree. Many of the cosmic symbols found in archaic religions reappear in these writings.

Native American Religion

I am using the word "religion" rather than "religions," even though I understand there are wide tribal variations among American Indians, because I want to focus on those aspects that are present in most of these variations.

Even some native Americans speak of "pan-Indianism" and emphasize "North American Religion" as an integrated system of beliefs and rituals. (40) I also understand that native Americans did not prefer the word "religion" but spoke simply of their "way of life". We use the word "religion" to speak of their way of life. In general, however, we can affirm, with Charlene Spretnak, that "on our continent the Native American nations have maintained unbroken practices of earth-based spirituality for more than twenty thousand years" (41) In his earlier books Richard Heinberg already anticipated the kinds of changes we need today. In *A New Covenant With Nature*, Heinberg emphasizes that "the practical wisdom of the world's primal peoples acquires ever-increasing importance as we seek to restore ecological balances that have lately been overwhelmed by the economic activities of civilization" (42)

We must begin by observing that the dominant culture, with its European roots, has repressed and, at times, tried to exterminate pagans, witches, the goddess, and indigenous people on this continent. According to many feminists this process began with the displacement of goddess religions in pre-literate cultures, and it continued with the horrible persecution in recent centuries of female healers who were thought to be witches. As for the native American people in North America, their population was at least one to two million (or probably around ten million) prior to the coming of the Europeans. The population of native Americans declined until the beginning of the twentieth century when it was down to about 269,388 in 1901, according to anthropologist Clark Wissler. (43) Although native American populations have been rebounding, it is obvious that they were nearly exterminated because white people of European descent wanted their land.

But the animus of whites against Indians goes beyond the taking of land. Frank Waters argues that "the deeply rooted racial prejudice of the Anglo-white Americans against the Red Indians, virtually a national psychosis, is one of the strangest and most terrifying phenomena in all history" (44) Evidence in support of such racism can be found in a collection of articles collected from newspapers in New York state between 1885 and 1910. (45) The fact that such intense efforts were made to also obliterate native cultures and traditions, by taking Indian children from their parents into residential schools, suggests that their religious values were somehow threatening to the dominant culture. The pagan and native American traditions embody values and a worldview that represent the recessive genes in our cultural organism. Jerry Mander shows a list about four pages long of the many ways in which Native American and European cultures differ. (46) Native American values represent an alternative to the dominant culture, and because they have been so forcibly repressed we can assume they are threatening. In addition, the survival of these recessive genes may remind the dominant culture that it carries a heavy burden of guilt, not only for its killing and cultural destruction, but also for its refusal to acknowledge a valuable alternative. Is it not common for people to suppress what they had repressed within themselves?

At the same time we must notice that these repressed traditions have also been romanticized and even glorified, and this is an ambivalent process. On the one hand there are, and always have been, some Americans who feel genuine admiration for those that the majority has suppressed. On the other hand, this romanticizing of the noble savage may be a way of controlling that which must be repressed by keeping it at a harmless distance in the past. Jerry Mander pointed out that advertising uses the image of the Indian in similar ways to valorize commercial products by associating them with the idealized image of the Indian. This process reduces the reality of the Indian to a "conceptual relic." (47) This prejudice is built into the language as we go "back to nature" or "back to the land" in movements that regress rather than progress. When reporters came to check out our School of Homesteading the title of their newspaper article might be something like "College Prof Brings Back the Good Old Days." This is a sentimental affirmation that denies any practical application or contemporary relevance.

While not all native American religions (or ways of life) are alike, they all venerate the land. The American Indian writer, Paula Gunn Allen, emphasizes this. "We are the land. To the best of my understanding, that is the fundamental idea that permeates American Indian life; the land (Mother) and the people (mothers) are the same . . . . The earth is the source and being of the people and we are equally the being of the earth." (48) Like nearly all indigenous people, native Americans feel they are part of Mother Earth and their myths of origin often are myths of emergence from the earth. They insist that land "is not a commodity that can be bought or sold, and to rip it open to mine it is deeply sacrilegious to all Indian people" (49) In a very succinct book calling for renewable energy, Winona LaDuke reviews examples of Native American opposition to coal and nuclear pollution on native lands in the West. (50)

At least some native Americans also recognized a magical Power, *Wakan-Tanka*, among the Sioux, *Manitou*, among the Algonquian, or *orenda*, among the Iroquois, which were sometimes referred to as Father or Grandfather and were sometimes also considered as Spirits. (51) After Christian missionaries did their work these other-than-human beings were also thought of as the Great Spirit, or God, since it was obvious to Indians that white people also had great Power.

Many Native Americans have expressed the belief that the world was created perfect. Mander quotes from the "A Basic Call to Consciousness" (1977) and the document opens as follows: "In the beginning we were told that human beings who walk about on the Earth have been provided with all things necessary for life" (52) Black Elk, an Oglala Sioux holy man or shaman, reports a vision he experienced which illustrates the nature of archetypes and repetition: "I looked about me and could see that what we then were doing was like a shadow cast upon the earth from yonder vision in the heavens, so bright it was and clear. I knew the real was yonder and the darkened dream of it was here" (53) Along with mystics from every tradition, Black Elk also emphasized that "everything an Indian does is in a circle, and that is because the Power of the World always works in circles, and everything tries to be round" (54) Again and again Black Elk refers to the Sacred Hoop, his image of the cosmos, which is divided into four quarters by lines symbolizing the four directions. Like most indigenous people, native Americans lived in cyclical time although the invasion of white people also made them painfully aware of the "terror of history." Thus Black Elk describes the Sun Dance, the ritual of cyclical regeneration which was held at the summer solstice, in chapter VIII of *Black Elk Speaks*, where it is sandwiched between accounts of battles with white soldiers.

Native American religion most clearly illustrates the proposition that religion is the substance of culture and culture is the form of religion. Throughout his book Mander mentions practical implications of Indian religions. Traditional Indians prefer a subsistence economy with barter over a cash economy. Goods are produced for use rather than for sale and ideally theirs is a steady state economy. While not all natives were farmers, the Hopi have been regarded as "the world's most proficient dry farmers," (55) a skill that may be of great value if climate change brings us droughts. Ake Hultkranz has argued that there are two types of native American religion: the hunters of the Plains and the horticultural tribes of which the Zuni are a typical example, along with the Hopi (56)

Native Americans have made other contributions to their conquerors. Mander takes nearly a whole chapter to explain how our concept of government was borrowed from the Iroquois Confederacy, (57) a fact that most citizens of the United States are too ignorant or too proud to acknowledge. Although there is much we have learned from the natives of this land, there is much more to learn.

I am aware that many native Americans have lost their traditional ways and yielded to the comfort and convenience of consumer goods. Other do maintain traditional ways, and it is these to whom white Americans may want to turn when it becomes necessary to do so. Many neo-pagans, who would seem to venerate Mother Earth, are similarly seduced by industrial products that have contributed to the destruction of the earth. It is the pattern of life-ways implicit in neo-pagans, goddess-worshipers and native Americans that we can affirm and try to embody after the era of cheap oil has ended and more of us are forced to return to living on the land.

An Australian neo-pagan philosopher, Val Plumwood, in reflecting on various kinds of spirituality, quotes a North American Indian writer who defined spirituality as being "inclined to honor, respect, and acknowledge the elements of our universe (both physical and nonphysical) that sustain and nourish our lives." (58) For Plumwood this implied a "materialistic spirituality" that helps us affirm our embodiment in the earth that nourishes and sustains us. She also raised questions about the notion of the sacred in this connection since too much emphasis on the sacred tends to perpetuate a matter/spirit dualism and undermines the reality that we must use that which we honor and respect. The challenge is to use it in sustainable ways while maintaining the sense of honor and respect.

CHAPTER IX

NAVIGATING THE CURRENTS
OF CULTURAL CHANGE

I intend that the title of this chapter be taken quite literally. As we begin to experience the new circumstances brought about by the end of cheap oil we will indeed be swept along in strong currents of cultural change. We will need all the navigational skills we can muster to steer our way through the rapids of change so that we arrive at a desirable place without crashing into the obstacles in the way.

Prospects for a Paradigm Shift.

David Korten's book of 2006, *The Great Turning*, subtitled *From Empire to Earth Community*, is a realistic encouragement to those who hope for fundamental change in America. It is realistic as it articulates its hope for a "turning" in the context of American history. People who postulate a change to a better future are merely wishful thinkers if their vision is not grounded in history. Korten's understanding of the reactionary forces (he calls them plutocrats and theocrats) that joined as the New Right to reestablish "Empire" after the liberating movements of the 1960s is especially illuminating. And, of course, the New Right culminated in the regime of the Bush Administration which is overtly seeking imperial control of scarce energy resources at the time of the end of oil. Korten considers the impact of the end of oil on this transition only very briefly. But his vision of the "Great Turning" and how it might happen is important as it presents another way of understanding the need and possibility of cultural transformation. In this book I am arguing that the process of cultural transformation will be forced on us by the end of oil, while Korten argues that the shift in cultural values is already under way as a result of choices that millions of people are making.

Korten was informed, in part, by a study published in 2000 under the title *The Cultural Creatives*. This study reports that there is a sub-culture of at least 50 or as many as 70 million citizens in the United States that emerged gradually in the latter part of the twentieth century from a wide variety of movements. They dissented as a counter-culture from the mainstream culture of modernism in America with its emphasis on materialistic and economic success. "Moderns" constitute a tradition that goes back to the Renaissance and the Scientific Revolution. The Moderns represent what I have called the dominant gene in our cultural organism. Cultural Creatives embody new spiritual and cultural values. About half of the Cultural Creatives are referred to as the Core Cultural Creatives who emphasize spiritual experience and the growth of consciousness. The other half are called the Green Cultural Creatives who share the environmental concerns of the Core group but with less emphasis on inner spiritual experience. The authors of the study suggest that because Cultural Creatives come out of such diverse backgrounds, they do not yet have a clear sense of themselves as a group with many compatible concerns. "It is as if they have had no mirror large and true enough to show them their own face." (1) (I have to say, however, that my experience in Green Politics, with its Ten Key Values, especially in the late 1980s and early 1990s, showed that Cultural Creatives could recognize each other in spite of their amazing diversity.)

This study of Cultural Creatives actually placed them in the context of two other sub-cultures: the Traditionals in addition to the Moderns. Traditionals emerged as part of a nineteenth century counter-culture, but their roots go deeper into the rural American distrust of urban industrialism. These are the people who invented Fundamentalism as a reaction to Modernism and include the New Right of today. In terms of numbers, which are bound to be inexact, the Moderns are 80 to 90 million, Traditionals about 48 million, and the Cultural Creatives at 50 to 70 million and growing. The authors point out that there are valuable contributions from all three groups. (2) My emphasis on agrarian values and local food movements, for example, is certainly an endorsement of traditional values as opposed to the centralizing tendency of modernism. But neo-agrarian values could also be seen as part of the Green Cultural Creatives.

In any case, the research on Cultural Creatives certainly supports my emphasis on the emergence of earth-centered spirituality as a significant influence in our culture at this time. Since traditional Christianity seems unable to recognize and challenge the demonic structure of Empire, it may be earth-centered spirituality that will emerge as the counter-force to demonic power. The values of Cultural Creatives, and especially their hope for cultural transformation, will help to make them willing to accept the changes needed as we adapt to the end of oil. I do see an impending conflict between Moderns and

Cultural Creatives. Moderns, who now control government and finance, either deny the end of oil or acknowledge it and ask how it might be possible to keep industrial civilization going with new energy technology and new fuels. Cultural Creatives, on the other hand, are likely to favor more modest energy-conserving lifestyles powered by decentralized sources of renewable energy. These might even include some "agrarian" aspects as alternatives to industrial modes of production, especially in relation to food.

But before we assume the battle is won, we need a clearer image of demonic power in our time. A repeated emphasis in this book has been the terrible and growing disparity of wealth and poverty all over the world and in the United States. Some consequences of this disparity have been brought into focus recently in the writing of Naomi Klein. She provides many examples of how the free market economic doctrines of Milton Friedman have destroyed governments (as in Chile) and national industries around the world (as in Asia) and replaced them with corporate entities mostly from the United States. These policies turned the "already wealthy into the super-rich and the organized working class into the disposable poor." (3) And, of course, this strategy, the "shock doctrine," is at work in this country too, especially after catastrophic events. Klein explains how this worked after 9/11. "What happened in the period of mass disorientation after the attacks was, in retrospect, a domestic form of economic shock therapy. The Bush team, Friedmanite to the core, quickly moved to exploit the shock that gripped the nation to push through its radical vision of a hollow government in which everything from war fighting to disaster response was a for-profit venture." (4) What Naomi Klein describes is the next step in the growth of demonic power as the fascist consortium of government and corporations does not hesitate to make war for profit. The result was "disaster capitalism" as the administration privatized various services that government used to perform. We therefore need to recognize that although a growing number of citizens, such as the Cultural Creatives, are yearning for change, they are opposed by those who are rich and powerful enough to control corporations and shape mass opinion. Those who work to preserve the earth as a human habitation are opposed by those who want to continue to profit from policies that destroy it.

David Ray Griffin emphasized that "the battle between divine and demonic power is therefore a real battle, with the outcome still undecided." (5) In terms of process thought, the evolution of life, as it culminated in human creativity, also gave rise to power based on selfishness and hate that can challenge the loving and compassionate intentions of divine power. In our culture, where money rules while the vast majority of people on the globe are impoverished, demonic power is clearly in charge—for now.

A paradigm can be defined as a model that shapes our perception of reality. The dominant paradigm in the Western world since "The Great Transformation," which made the market economy normative, is economic—the "bottom line" is what counts. So far the business community has responded to the energy crisis in its usual way, as a marketing opportunity. Our religion is the religion of the shopping mall. Of course this is not true for all of us, but it remains the paradigm for most consumers and for business and government, the institutions that shape our reality. In the long run this paradigm may change when enough people have changed and put pressure on these governing institutions. I mentioned, at the end of Chapter II, a few of the reasons for expecting a basic change in our cultural values. And in Chapter III I reviewed a series of needed changes that would, if put into practice, add up to a paradigm shift. Most of these changes are possible as choices people can make in how they live. I argued that those changes are necessary if we as a society are to adapt to the end of oil in an orderly manner. Now we need to consider the likelihood that these changes, along with changes in our religious and spiritual values, could occur on a political level.

Many writers on peak oil project a cataclysmic view regarding the future of industrial civilization, but it is important to remember that some see the possibility of an orderly transition, a kind of paradigm shift. Already in response to the energy crisis of the 1970s, W. Jackson Davis pointed to some of the positive aspects of a post-industrial society: a rebirth of community, more meaningful work, a more decentralized government, and the recovery of a relationship to nature as more people move to rural areas. He held out the promise that "the decline of one civilization promises the birth of another, more advanced civilization." (6)

More recently Howard T. and Elizabeth C. Odum published *A Prosperous Way Down*. Based on their work on the analysis of energy systems, the Odums seem almost optimistic about the future and express confidence that society as a system adapts to availability or limitations of energy. They argue for the possibility of social change in a fairly sudden way on the basis of a "pulsing paradigm" which can explain how society can accept new ways. "As change occurs, individuals begin to think about what is different and a general shared feeling builds up gradually in the society. Then at some threshold the new idea jumps into the forefront of social discourse, and most people's attitudes flip together." (7) This would constitute a paradigm shift in a society. The shift to smaller families is suggested as an example of this sudden social change, and the Odums repeatedly emphasize the fact that population must decrease at the rate that energy resources decrease. Unfortunately they are vague about the temporal correlation of population and resources. In fact, of course, population is still growing even as we are on the verge of peak oil. The Odums appear to have faith in self-regulating mechanisms: "Human society can adapt to diminishing resources in ways analogous to ecosystems. To sustain standards of living, populations will have to decrease. People will either adapt because of foresight or will be forced to because of declining resources." (8) In their view social change is not only possible; it is inevitable.

One of the things that has encouraged me to raise the possibility that change can be accepted in a pluralistic society has grown out of my experiences with organic farmers for over thirty years. Very few of these had always been organic farmers; nearly all started as conventional farmers who used some chemicals. Some switched to organic methods because they had suffered from pesticide poisoning. Some switched for environmental reasons, as I did. Some switched because they felt nature was sacred while their neighbors switched because they wanted to be good Christian stewards. And some, especially in recent years, are hoping to make more money by producing for the organic market. But I have noticed that after these farmers practice organic farming methods of working in harmony with nature for a few years they move from an anthropocentric orientation to a biocentric orientation. And this move is on a practical level long before it is recognized and takes shape on an intellectual level. This is a very common experience. As we recycle we gradually recognize that environmental sinks for waste are finite, as the earth is. As gasoline becomes too costly for us to use for pleasure in our cars we can easily move to the idea that it is a good idea to drive less and reduce the emissions of carbon dioxide.

When we as a nation face common problems it is possible to act in a unified manner in spite of fundamental differences. Many Evangelicals are affirming "Creation Care" in the religious terms they find congenial. Korten provides evidence that the roughly 30 million Evangelicals in this country are probably evenly divided between those who live by the ecological values that are those of the emerging Earth Community and those that support the New Right with its emphasis on the values of Empire. (9)

The shift from an economic to an ecological paradigm may already be under way on a popular level. At this time, however, we, as a society, want both; we want to have our cake, a clean environment and a functioning ecosystem, and we want to eat it too with more affluence and consumer goods. Given the tremendous power of advertising, this is not surprising. We are constantly bombarded by the propaganda of very large corporations and many of us are held in a cultural trance. It is not easy for people to see through corporate propaganda or advertising. Some corporations even practice "green-washing" as they falsely associate their activities with environmental causes. But the very widespread association of religious values and ecology, which is already happening in virtually all religious traditions and denominations, including many evangelical traditions, is helping to sensitize people to a new spirituality. Theologian Mark I. Wallace emphasizes the transforming role of the Holy Spirit: "Throughout the Bible, the Spirit is the divine agent for radical social change." (10) It is my hope that this book can contribute to the cultivation of the ecology/religion garden by fostering the growth of helpful plants and pruning the old growth.

But once we recognize that our lives are colonized by the combination of government and corporate power, we know that there can be no cultural transformation until we are freed from that power over us. In other words, all our good efforts to liberate ourselves by choosing to live in more self-reliant and sustainable ways must be supported by efforts toward decolonization. This two-fold process of social change was articulated several years ago by James Robertson. (11) In our time it is the multi-national corporations who have the wealth and power to control government as they lobby for policies that assure continued economic growth, profit for themselves, and revenue for government. Some critics of corporate activity, such as Thom Hartmann, might see this as fascism: "a system of government that exercises a dictatorship of the extreme right, typically through a merging of state and business leadership, together with belligerent nationalism." (12) In our time this unholy alliance has been reinforced by the Religious Right. The corporate control of the media gives them the power to shape public opinion so that many people have seen corporate activities as being in the public interest. It is possible, however, that the war in Iraq, and the policies it unleashed, allows more and more people to recognize it as another war for profit and to see that the USA is moving toward fascism. Although writers like David Korten have been providing evidence that corporate influence is waning, the fact that corporations continue to exercise power testifies to the fact that we do live in an authoritarian fascist state.

David Korten on the waning of corporate power.
Nearly three out of four Americans (72 percent) believe corporations have too much power over too many aspects of American life. Clearly distinguishing between big and small businesses, 74 percent say big companies have too much influence over government policy and politicians; 82 percent say small business has too little. Eighty eight percent distrust corporate executives, and 90 percent want new corporate regulations and tougher enforcement of existing laws. Only 4 percent believe that America is best served when corporations pursue only one goal—making the most profit for their shareholders. Ninety five percent believe corporations should sacrifice some profit for the sake of making things better for their workers and communities. (13)

Moving Beyond Fascism

Although corporate influence and prestige may be waning, their power remains strong. How can the power of corporations over our lives be broken? One way, which several non-profit groups are working on, is to get local governments to revoke corporate charters, or at least to ban them from local areas. (14) Because of corporate power this is difficult to the point of impossible, but it has had limited success. Another way is to work on a political level to choose a party on a national level, such as the Greens, that will control corporate activity. This is difficult because the two main parties are bought and paid for by big business, and so far they have kept third parties in a very distant third place. And it is difficult because many people still believe that corporations serve us with the economic growth they exemplify. But, as Michael Lerner has very recently reminded us, politics does sometimes move in unexpected ways, and given the crisis brought on by the ill-advised war in Iraq, we may be at a time when there is an opening for new initiatives. In his book *The Left Hand of God: Taking Back our Country from the Religious Right*, Rabbi Lerner is calling for an interfaith "Network of Spiritual Progressives" (NEP) that would work to bring spiritual values into a politics that could appeal to people on the Left, and this is being organized. He correctly sees the Right as a politics based on fear; the Left could be a politics based on hope. And there is no question that the NEP will work to curtail the power of corporations and to develop a more caring and ecological society.

There is still another way in which the power of corporations can be broken so that our society could move beyond economic growth into planning for the end of oil. Corporations are creating a suicide economy; many of them will be unable to survive in the future because everything they do is so energy-intensive. Remember that economic growth is like the ideology of the cancer cell which intends to grow until it consumes its host. If people cannot pay the higher prices that expensive energy will create, and instead develop alternatives as outlined above in chapter III, the power of corporations, already weakened, will erode further and their prestige will evaporate. On the other hand, of course, it seems very likely that corporations will try to control the development of renewable energy, as agri-businesses like Cargill and Archer Daniels Midland are already hoping to profit from the development of biofuels like ethanol to supplement gasoline. They will do everything they can to perpetuate the continuation of industrial society, even if they thereby increase the rate and intensity of global warming, as the production of oil from ethanol and tar sands is already doing.

It is also important to recognize the fact that some corporate survival may be helpful in the years ahead to secure the stabilization of society, even as corporations do this in their own self-interest. They may see that they can survive only as they self-transform into more benevolent and truly energy-conserving organizations. If this sounds too good to be true, it probably is, but it is possible. During the energy crisis of the Seventies electric utilities changed their role from mere producers and distributors of energy to promotion of conservation practices and more efficient use. This did not last long, but in another crisis it could happen again, and with the option to buy "green" electric energy from small-scale producers with net metering, the first steps have been taken.

The more likely and democratic way to change is through a government that tries to serve the needs of the people and the long-term needs of the planet. Richard Heinberg's promotion of the oil depletion protocol (discussed at the end of Chapter II above) would serve this function. It would be the sane alternative to international anarchism. This can happen, especially if the bankrupt policies of the current Bush administration are thoroughly discredited. This administration, blinded by absolute military power, seems unable to change its course as it tries to use military power for its access to oil, and it will fail. One way to imagine this failure is to recognize that the privatization of governmental services is extremely costly. The people who are being asked to pay for these services are increasingly impoverished. As the cost of energy rises, they will be even less able to continue to buy the goods and services that corporations have to sell. As corporations try to get all the wealth for themselves they will discover that the people can no longer buy their products. Corporations appear to be so blinded by power, so immune to negative feedback, that they ignore the changing circumstances that will destroy them. Once they assume absolute power, which absolves them from relationship, they embrace their fatal weakness.

In the final analysis I am convinced that it is the people who will demand freedom from corporate control and a fundamental reversal in energy and economic policy—but not until our situation verges on severe deprivation. We began this discussion of the possibility of social change at the end of Chapter II and suggested that serious negative feedback loops, such as the end of cheap oil, or global warming, might prompt people to move away from the dominant paradigm. If present political policies continue to impoverish more of the middle class we will soon be a society in which the large majority will be suffering real poverty, especially as energy prices rise, along with the prices of the many things that require oil in their manufacture. When those who have enjoyed the benefits of affluence are denied what they have been accustomed to, we can expect widespread dissatisfaction and cultural unrest. Once it becomes clear that the government cannot bring back cheap oil, there will be high levels of frustration. We can expect that the few voices calling for a reversal in energy and economic policies will be joined by more and more voices. As Korten put it, "the birthing of Earth Community begins with liberating the mind from the tyranny of the belief that there is no alternative to Empire." (15) A sensible federal government would hear these voices and lead the nation in an orderly transition to a steady-state economy. Surely this should be a possibility for Homo Sapiens, if we are truly wise, as our species name implies.

The Risky Possibility of Cultural Revitalization

If a deep cultural transition to a new ecological paradigm can occur in this rational and democratic manner, as writers like David Korten suggest, we would be extremely fortunate. But if we recognize that we are already in the grip of a fascist system that profits from catastrophe, it might be foolish to expect corporations to forego the profits promised by coming disasters. We can expect that our individual choices, and the collective decisions of the people, will be opposed or frustrated by corporations seeking profit from the catastrophic events that are likely to accompany the end of oil and/or global warming. Change is therefore likely to happen in less predictable ways as the cultural organism transforms itself. As the stress suffered by more and more individuals becomes unbearable, symptoms of cultural distortion will become visible. Once that point is reached we can expect a revitalization movement that could have revolutionary consequences. Anthropologists who have studied such movements, which recur in various times and places, have generated a considerable literature describing the causes of, and stages in, revitalization or millenarian movements. In some cases a revitalization movement follows from a sudden disaster, a possibility that is articulated by Michael Barkun in his book *Disaster and the Millennium*. The kind of disaster we can envision might happen if oil, or food, was suddenly so high in price that they would be unaffordable, and this could trigger a revitalization movement. But a revitalization movement can also occur as a result of a long and difficult period of stress, anxiety or discomfort in a society. A classic and concise paper on the subject that is frequently cited is "Revitalization Movements" by Anthony F. C. Wallace.

Wallace defined a revitalization movement "as a deliberate, organized, conscious effort by members of a society to construct a more satisfying culture." He distinguished five over-lapping stages in the process: 1. Steady State, 2. Period of Individual Stress, 3. Period of Cultural Distortion, 4. Period of Revitalization, and 5. New Steady State. When a substantial number of individuals in a society feel increasing levels of stress they begin to feel that their "mazeway" is disintegrating. The mazeway is a model or mental image or paradigm, and it disintegrates when it no longer makes sense because it no longer works. In our situation the old mazeway could be seen as the cluster of ideas and values that support the notion of economic growth in an industrial system, our dominant paradigm. A mazeway includes images of nature, society, culture, personality and physical environment, all tied into one complex model. When the mazeway no longer makes sense and causes stress, a person may want to change the mazeway, which in our case might be the shift to an ecological paradigm. Let me quote Wallace here:

"Changing the mazeway involves changing the total Gestalt of his image of self, society, and culture, of nature and body, and of ways of action. It may also be necessary to make changes in the 'real' system in order to bring mazeway and 'reality' into congruence. The effort to work a change in mazeway and 'real' system together so as to permit more effective stress reduction is the effort at revitalization; and the collaboration of a number of persons in such an effort is called a revitaliztion movement." (16) Even though many individuals may change their mazeway, the changes in the 'real' world may be resisted by powerful persons and institutions with a vested interest in the old steady state, and this would frustrate those ready for change and cause more stress. As a result of increased stress, the society begins to move into the period of cultural distortion as people fall into regressive behaviours such as "alcoholism, extreme passivity and indolence, the development of highly ambivalent dependency relationships, intragroup violence, disregard of kinship and sexual mores, irresponsibility of public officials," etc (17) Given these symptoms, we may already be entering the period of cultural distortion in our society.

It is this stage, when the cultural organism begins acting out, that makes social change through a revitalization movement so risky. A culture could disintegrate under this increased stress caused by internal cultural distortion. Not every revitalization movement succeeds. In the Ghost Dance of the 1880s, some who danced fell into a trance in which they saw visions of the earth as it was before the white people came. Black Elk participated in the Ghost Dances and in one of his visions he saw a holy shirt which, he believed, would protect the wearer. Many shirts were made and worn in the belief that they would make the wearer invulnerable to bullets. Thus the Sioux were emboldened to fight the soldiers who were disarming them, and the result was the Wounded Knee Massacre on December 29, 1890 in which 60 soldiers and about 200 native men, women and children were killed. (18) The Ghost Dance provided visions of a new earth, but there was no change in the reality of the Sioux as a defeated people confined to a reservation.

The rise of the Religious Right to power in this country can also be seen as a failing revitalization movement. It has all the apocalyptic energy of a revitalization movement as it sees this as a time of crisis, and it has a vision of a new earth, but its vision of our old world is blinkered because is based on denial. According to Kevin Phillips in *American Theocracy*, it denies decisive aspects of the old world: it denies the end of oil, it denies climate change, it denies economic decline and debt. Moreover, given the millennial expectations in the Fundamentalism of the Religious Right, it is fair to assume that the New Earth it envisions is the thousand-year Reign of Christ after the Rapture. And, as writers such as David Domke and Kevin Phillips have shown, the Religious Right has a theocratic vision that is at odds with our democratic traditions. (19) Moreover, even the new earth it envisions is a mythic projection as described in the Book of Relevation. It is not a viable revitalization movement.

When a revitalization movement succeeds it may be because a visionary or charismatic prophet emerges to articulate a new and acceptable mazeway, as Handsome Lake did for the Seneca when he was given visions starting in 1799 that successfully revived the tribe. (20) We can imagine a scenario in which Al Gore, for example, follows the momentum of his success with *An Inconvenient Truth*, and perhaps other publications on global warming, with the successful promotion of an oil depletion protocol. Let us also imagine other social circumstances which shape public opinion, such as the failure of U. S. military attempts to secure access to oil, exorbitant prices for oil and the economic hardship that creates, along with widespread disenchantment with both of the major political parties. Add to this factors such as the popular acceptance of prophecies from native American and/or astrological calculations which reveal that fateful cosmic events will destroy humankind in 2012 unless the correct decisions are made. In this context Al Gore is drafted to run for the presidency as a Green in 2011, or, better yet, because he seems to be a pragmatic Old Boy politician who has not yet given much evidence that he shares the cluster of values that would be necessary for a real transformation, he is drafted to run as Vice President with, let's say, Winona LaDuke as the candidate for President. Gore has national visibility, but LaDuke, as a native American woman who has written about renewable energy and been active in Green politics, embodies the values that would appeal to an electorate that wants to see a transformation. Although our history makes all this improbable, it is not impossible in about 2012, and it would foster a cultural revitalization.

Or sometimes enough people in the society already see an acceptable new mazeway, as may be the case in our situation with the emergence of 50 million (or more) Cultural Creatives most able and willing to adapt to the new cultural and spiritual situation at the end of oil. The spiritual values we have considered in this book are shared by many. Sometimes, as was suggested in Chapter VI, the collective vision of a new earth by a generation may inspire the actual building of that new earth. Scholars, such as William G. McLaughlin, have tried to show that we have been in a revitalization process since the 1960s, that it began to bear fruit in the 1970s, and that it was set back by the Reaganite counter-revolution. (21) Now, as the dissatisfactions continue to grow and the evidence of stress is all around us, some of the Cultural Creatives may lead the way. And, as I have tried to show, the old steady state, or mazeway, or economic paradigm, and the new mazeway, the ecological paradigm, each has disparate elements that add up to a couple of sets of integrated systems which are in opposition to each other.

As the religious and spiritual alternatives promoted in this book continue to grow, those people attracted to them will find their passage into the new paradigm a kind of natural next step. Others will find the mazeway based on the ecological paradigm makes sense. In the transitional period we will see much contention and disagreement. We are talking about a change so massive and complex that it will be difficult to coordinate all the aspects of the transition, especially if the change is not made rationally and deliberately before the stress creates cultural distortion. This transformation is not for single issue thinkers or reformers. But we can have confidence that the new ecological paradigm has enough organic integrity that its parts will fit together (as Chapter III tried to show) even if the cultural organism has to transform itself, so to speak, in a revitalization movement.

But will the conflicts over the end of cheap oil really escalate into a revitalization movement? We have followed a logical progression to its end point and this scenario of revitalization is certainly a possibility. Other scenarios are also possible. If the rising prices of energy are slow and gradual, so that we, as individuals and as a society, have time to adjust, and if economic collapse is also gradual, it is likely that societal collapse might be, as Joseph Tainter argued, a shift from a more complex to a less complex society. As more people are resettled in rural areas, where they have the opportunity to raise food as small-scale farmers, we could see a shift from an industrial to a neo-agrarian society. This possibility has been argued throughout this book, but it may also be seen as an inevitability. As energy becomes too expensive to support industrial methods of affordable food production, processing, distribution, and transportation from other countries, people quite naturally turn to local production. And this leads the way toward an agrarian society. But it will be an orderly process only if there is a political process of decolonization. At some point politicians will have to recognize that it is counter-productive to support and subsidize corporations with their energy-intensive industrial methods and instead support and subsidize land redistribution to small farmers. At that point the shift to a neo-agrarian society will have begun.

In Chapter III we noticed that Cuba managed a partial transition to an agrarian society so that people could be fed. And Dmitry Orlov, in a recent book comparing the collapse of the Soviet Union with the coming economic collapse in the United States, suggested that the collapse in the Soviet Union was not too difficult for citizens because, despite the collectivization of agriculture, private plots were productive enough to provide food and people were guaranteed housing. Unfortunately, housing is not guaranteed in the United States and the many backyard gardens do not provide enough food. Thus Orlov concludes that "the Soviet Union was much better prepared for economic collapse than is the United States." But he also emphasizes that the collapse is slow in the United States, "a steady erosion of quality of life for most people." (22) If so, Americans can indeed adapt to the end of oil. Activities in the home and community will be increasingly important, and if these activities are carried out on the land, it can be a joyful homecoming. The collapse can thus be a soft landing rather than a crash.

ENDNOTES

INTRODUCTION

1. John Dominic Crossan, *Jesus: A Revolutionary Biography* (San Francisco: Harper, 1995.)
2. Jim Wallis, *God's Politics* (San Francisco: Harper, 2005), chapter 13.

CHAPTER I

1. Richard Heinberg, *The Party's Over* (Gabriola Island: New Society Publishers, 2005), 101-136.
2. Colin Campbell, *The Coming Oil Crisis* (Brentwood, Essex, England: Multi-science Publications & Petroconsultants, 1997). 73.
3. Matthew R. Simmons, *Twilight in the Desert* (New York: John Wiley & Sons, 2005), 349.
4. Peter Tertzakian, *A Thousand Barrels a Second* (New York: McGraw Hill, 2006), 129.
5. Richard Heinberg, *The Oil Depletion Protocol* (Gabriola Island: New Society Publishers, 2006), 25.
6. David and Marcia Pimentel, *Food, Energy and Society* (New York: John Wiley, 1996), 13, 27.
7. John Gever, et. al., *Beyond Oil* (Cambridge, MA: Ballinger Publishing Co., 1986), 13, 27.
8. Daniel Yergin, *The Prize* (New York: Simon & Schuster, 1991), Chapters 29, 30, 31.
9. Andrew Bacevich, *The New American Militarism* (New York: Oxford University Press, 2005), 103, 182.
10. Heinberg, *The Party's Over*, 95.
11. Michael Ruppert, *Crossing the Rubicon* (Gabriola Island: New Society Publishers, 2004), 82-87, 575.
12. David Ray Griffin, *The New Pearl Harbor* (Northampton, MA: Olive Branch Press, 2004).

13. Michael Klare, *Resource Wars*. (New York: Henry Holt & Co., 2001), 2-3, 62-68. See also Chalmers Johnson, *The Sorrows of Empire* (New York: Metropolitan Books, 2004), chapter 6.
14. Paul and Anne Ehrlich, *The End of Affluence* (New York: Ballantine Books, 1974), 51.
15. Richard Heinberg, *Powerdown*. (Gabriola Island: New Society Publishers, 2004), 74-75.
16. Heinberg, *The Party's Over*, 230.
17. Howard T. Odum, "The Ecosystem, Energy, and Human Values," *Zygon: Journal of Religion and Science*, 12 (June, 1977), 132.
18. Heinberg, *Powerdown*, 25, 34-37.
19. Pimentel, *Food, Energy and Society*, 27.
20. William R. Catton, *Overshoot* (Urbana, IL: University of Illinois Press, 1980), 3.
21. Michael Pollan, *The Omnivore's Dilemma* (New York: Penguin Press, 2006), 43.
22. George Pyle, *Raising Less Corn, More Hell* (New York: Public Affairs, 2005), 103.
23. Matt Savinar, *The Oil Age is Over* (Kearney, NE: Morris Publishing, 2005), 11.
24. Pollan, *The Omnivore's Dilemma*, 43.
25. These issues were also discussed by Robert Stivers, *The Sustainable Society* (Philadelphia: The Westminster Press, 1976), chapter 7.
26. Donella Meadows, et. al., *Beyond the Limits* (Vermont: Chelsea Green Publishing Co., 1992), 77-78.
27. Donella Meadows, et. al., *Limits to Growth: The Thirty Year Update* (Vermont: Chelsea Green Publishing Co., 2004), 91, 115-120.
28. Simmons, *Twilight in the Desert*, 346
29. Ruppert, *Crossing the Rubicon*, 561
30. Barbara Kingsolver, *Animal, Vegetable, Miracle* (New York: HarperCollins, 2007), 20
31. Campbell, *The Coming Oil Crisis*, 115.
32. Julian Darley, *High Noon for Natural Gas* (Vermont: Chelsea Green P:ublishing Co., 2004), 123.
33. William R. Clark, *Petrodollar Warfare* (Gabriola Island: New Society Publishers, 2005), 31, chapter 5.
34. William Ophuls and A Stephan Boyan, *Ecology and the Politics of Scarcity Revisited* (New York: W. H. Freeman & Co., 1992), 237-238, 283.
35. Quoted in *ibid*, 197.

CHAPTER II

1. William R. Catton, *Overshoot* (Urbana, IL: University of Illinois Press, 1980), xv.
2. Mircea Eliade, "Paradise and Utopia: Mythological Geography and Eschatology," in *The Quest* (Chicago: University of Chicago Press, 1969), chapter 6.
3. Karl Lowith, *Meaning in History* (Chicago: University of Chicago Press, 1957), 111.
4. Mircea Eliade, *Cosmos and History* (New York: Harper Torchbooks, 1959), 107

5. Lynn White, Jr., "The Historical Roots of our Ecologic Crisis," in *The Subversive Science*, edited by Paul Shepard and Daniel McKinley (New York: Houghton Mifflin Company, 1969), 346.

6. Susan Griffin, *Woman and Nature* (New York: Harper and Row, 1978), and Rosemary Radford Ruether, *New Woman, New Earth* (New York: Seabury :Press, 1975).

7. Lowith, *Meaning in History*, 192.

8. Robert Bellah, et. al., *Habits of the Heart* (New York: Harper & Row, 1985), 143.

9. Lowith, *Meaning in History*, 192.

10. Lewis Mumford, *Techniques and Civilization* (New York: Harcourt, Brace and World, 1963), 36-40.

11. Carolyn Merchant, *The Death of Nature* (San Francisco: Harper & Row, 1980), 170.

12. David Noble, *The Religion of Technology* (New York: Alfred A. Knopf, 1998), 49.

13. David Korten, *The Post-Corporate World* (San Francisco: Barrett-Koehler, 1999), 116.

14. Rene Dubos, *A God Within* (New York: Charles Scribner's Sons, 1972), 264.

15. E. F. Schumacher, *Small is Beautiful* (New York: Harper Torchbooks, 1973), 138-139, 143.

16. Scott Burns, *Home, Inc.* (Garden City, NY: Doubleday & Company, 1975), 75.

17. Herman Daly and John Cobb, *For the Common Good* (Boston: Beacon Press, 1989), 139.

18. Richard Heinberg, *The Party's Over* (Gabriola Island: New Society Publishers, 2005), 187-189, and Julian Darley, *High Noon for Natural Gas* (Vermont: Chelsea Green Publishing Co. 2004), 175-179.

19. Eric Davis, *TechGnosis* (New York: Crown Publishers, 2004), 189.

20. William Ophuls and A. Stephan Boyan, *Ecology and the Politics of Scarcity Revisited* (New York: W. H. Freeman & Co, 1992), 106.

21. Lester Brown, *Outgrowing the Earth* (New York: W. W. Norton, 2004), 130.

22. David Ray Griffin, *Christian Faith and the Truth Behind 9/11* (Louisville: Westminster John Knox Press, 2006), 175-180.

23. Norman O. Brown, *Life Against Death* (New York: Vintage Books, 1959), 240.

24. Karl Polanyi, *The Great Transformation* (Boston: Beacon P:ress, 1957), 57.

25. *Ibid*, 42.

26. Barry Commoner, *The Closing Circle* (New York: Bantam Books, 1972), 151.

27. Ivan Illich, *Shadow Work* (Boston: Marion Boyers, 1986), 57-58.

28. Ivan Illich, *Toward a History of Needs* (New York: Pantheon Books, 1978), 39.

29. Richard J. Barnet, *The Lean Years* (New York: Simon & Schuster, 1980), 258.

30. David Korten, *When Corporations Rule the World* (Hartford, CT: Kumarian Press and San Francisco: Berrett-Koehler, 1997), 107.

31. Gar Alperwitz, "Another World is Possible," *Mother Jones*, (January-February, 2006) 69.

32. Daly and Cobb, *For the Common Good*, 204.
33. J. Matthew Sleeth, *Serve God, Save the Planet* (Vermont: Chelsea Green Publishing Co., 2006), 30-31.
34. Wendell Berry, "The Agrarian Standard," in *The Essential Agrarian Reader*, edited by Norman Wirzba (Lexington: University of Kentucky Press, 2003), 29.
35. Paul H. Ray and Sherry Ruth Anderson, *The Cultural Creatives* (New York: Three Rivers Press, 2000).
36. Richard Heinberg, *The Oil Depletion Protocol* (Gabriola Island: New Society : Publishers, 2006), xi.

CHAPTER III

1. Wendell Berry, *The Unsettling of America* (San Francisco: Sierra Club Books, 1977), 87.
2. Herman Daly and John Cobb, *For the Common Good* (Boston: Beacon Press, 1989), 390.
3. Bill Devall and George Sessions, *Deep Ecology* (Salt Lake City: Peregrine Smith Books, 1985), 66-69.
4. Herman Daly, "Introduction to a Steady State Economy," in *Economics, Ecology, Ethics* (San Francisco: W. H. Freeman & Co., 1980), 10.
5. *Ibid*, 324-325.
6. David and Marcia Pimentel, *Food, Energy, and Society* (New York: John Wiley, 1996), 13.
7. See Edward Renshaw, *The End of Progress* (Boston: Duxbury Press, 1976), 66-67.
8. Karl Peters, "Realities and Ideals in the World System," *Zygon: Journal of Religion and Science, 12* (June, 1977), 169.
9. Daly, "Introduction to a Steady State Economy," 330ff.
10. Herman Daly and Joshua Farley, *Ecological Economics* (Washington, DC: Island Press, 2004), 249.
11. Margrit Kennedy, *Interest and Inflation Free Money* (Okemos, MI: Seva International, 1995), chapter 1.
12. David Ray Griffin, *Christian Faith and the Truth Behind 9/11* (Louisville, KY: Westminster John Knox Press, 2006), 174.
13. Kennedy, *Interest and Inflation Free Money*, 56.
14. Daly and Farley, *Ecological Economics*, 255-256.
15. Thomas Greco, Jr., *New Money for Healthy Communities* (Tucson, AZ: by author, 1994) 88-95, 117-129.
16. Bernard Lietaer, *The Future of Money* (London: Century, 2001), 125-212. *http://www.berkshares.org*.
17. James Robertson, *Future Wealth* (New York: Bootstrap Press, 1990), 125-127.
18. Kennedy, *Interest and Inflation Free Money*, 35-42.
19. Alfredo de Romano, "The Autonomous Economy" *Interculture*, XXVV (Summer and Fall, 1989, Issues 104 and 105), Part I, 56.

20. James Robertson, *Future Work* (New York: Universe Books, 1985), chapters 3 and 11.
21. Berry, *The Unsettling of America*, 82.
22. Tom Bender, quoted by Lane de Moll and Gigi Coe, editors, *Stepping Stones* (New York: Schocken Books, 1978), 73.
23. E. F. Schumacher, *Small is Beautiful* (New York: Harper Torchbooks, 1973), 161ff.
24. Donella Meadows, et. al., *Limits to Growth: The Thirty Year Update* (Vermont: Chelsea Green Publishing Co, 2004), 96.
25. Karl Polanyi, *The Great Transformation* (Boston: Beacon Press, 1957), 71.
26. Berry, *The Unsettling of America*, chapter 4.
27. David Orr, *Earth in Mind* (Washington, DC: Island Press, 1994), 187.
28. Richard Heinberg, *The Oil Depletion Protocol* (Gabriola Island: New Society Publishers, 2006), 119.
29. Brian Donahue, *Reclaiming the Commons* (New Haven: Yale University Press, 1999).
30. Orr, *Earth in Mind*, p. 173.
31. Starhawk, *The Earth Path* (San Francisco: Harper, 2004), 117.
32. D. A. Crosley, et. al., "The Positive Interactions in Agroecosystems," in *Agricultural Ecosystems*, edited by R. Lowrance, et. al. (New York: John Wiley, 1984).
33. Richard Heinberg, *Powerdown* (Gabriola Island: New Society Publishers, 2004), 184.
34. Orr, *Earth In Mind*, 173-178.
35. See J. Jenkins, *The Humanure Book*.
36. Wes Jackson, *Alters of Unhewn Stone* (San Francisco: North Point Press, 1987), 106-146.
37. Joseph Tainter, *The Collapse of Complex Societies* (Cambridge: Cambridge University Press), 31, 215.
38. Jay Marhoefer, *Re-Energizing America* (Livermore, CA: Wingspan Press, 2007).
39. Amory Lovins, *Soft Energy Paths* (New York: Harper Colophon Books, 1979), 40.
40. Pimentel, *Food, Energy and Society*, chapter 19.
41. Stephan Harding, *Animate Earth* (Foxhole, Dartington, Tontes, Devon: Green Books, 2006), 191.
42. *Ibid.*, 194.
43. Elizabeth Kolbert, *Field Notes from Catastrophe* (New York: Bloomsbury Publishing, 2006), 131-147.
44. Ted Nordhaus and Michael Shellenberger, *Break Through* (Boston: Houghton Mifflin Company, 2007), 113.

CHAPTER IV

1. Pimentel, *Food, Energy and Society*, 261.
2. John Berger, *Pig Earth* (New York: Pantheon, 1979), 210.

3. Garret Hardin, "Carrying Capacity as an Ethical Concept," in *Lifeboat Ethics*, edited by George R. Lucas and Thomas Ogletree (New York: Harper Forum Books, 1976), 138.

4. Joseph Fletcher, "Feeding the Hungry: An Ethical Appraisal," *Ibid.*, 60.

1. Paul Tillich, *Theology of Culture* (New York: Galaxy Books, 1964), 42.

2. See Shayne Lee, "Prosperity Theology: T. D. Jakes and the Gospel of the Almighty Dollar," *Cross Currents* 57 (Summer 2007), 227-236.

3. Harvey Cox, *Fire From Heaven* (Reading, PA: Addison Wesley Publishing, 1995), 258.

CHAPTER V

1. Richard Heinberg, *A New Covenant with the Earth* (Wheaton, IL: Quest Books, 1996), 129.

2. Obery M. Hendricks, *The Politics of Jesus* (New York: Doubleday, 2006), 334.

3. John B. Cobb, et. al., *The American Empire and the Commonwealth of God* (Louisville, KY: Westminster John Knox Press, 2006), 142.

4. Robert N. Bellah, "Civil Religion in America," in *American Civil Religion*, edited by Russell E. Richey and Donald G. Jones (New York: Harper & Row, 1974), 40.

5. Bill Devall, *Living Richly in an Age of Limits* (Salt Lake City: Gibbs Smith, 1993), chapter 1.

6. Max Weber, *The Protestant Ethic and the Spirit of Capitalism*, (New York: Charles Scribner's Sons, 1958), 115.

7. Gordon Kaufman, "Response to Elizabeth A. Johnson," in *Christianity and Ecology*, edited by Rosemary Radford Ruether and Dieter Hessel (Cambridge: Harvard University Press, 2000), 24.

8. Leonardo Boff and Phillip Berryman, *Cry of the Earth, Cry of the Poor* (Maryknoll, NY: Orbis Books, 1997), 78-81.

9. Thom Hartmann, *The Last Hours of Ancient Sunlight* (New York: Three Rivers Press, 2004), 155.

10. Michael Specter, "Political Science," *The New Yorker* (March 13, 2006). 64.

11. Tony Campolo, *Speaking my Mind* (Nashville, TN: W Publishing Group, 2004), 206.

12. Kevin Phillips, *American Theocracy* (New York: Viking Penguin, 2006), 252-255.

13. *Ibid.*, 217.

14. Matthew Fox, *Creation Spirituality* (San Francisco: Harper, 1991), 99-100.

15. David Domke, *God Willing?* (London & Ann Arbor: Pluto Press, 2004), 181-183.

16. Seymour Martin Lipset, *American Exeptionalism* (New York: W. W. Norton, 1996), 61-62.

17. Matthew Fox, *Original Blessing* (Santa Fe: Bear & Co., 1983), 11.

18. David Ray Griffin, *Christian Faith and the Truth Behind 9/11* (Louisville, KY: Westminster John Knox Press, 2006). 137, 144.

19. See Nicholas Berdyaev, *Truth and Revelation* (New York: Collier Books, 1962), 122

20. Valerie Saiving, "The Human Situation: A Feminist View" in *Womanspirit Rising*, edited by Carol Christ and Judith Plaskow (San Francisco: Harper & Row, 1979), 25-42.

21. Ivone Gebara, quoted by Rosemary Radford Ruether in "Ecofeminism: the Challenge to Theology, in *Christianity and Ecology*, edited by Ruether and Hessel, 105.

CHAPTER VI

1. Tom Hayden, *The Lost Gospel of the Earth* (San Francisco: Sierra Club Books, 1996), 60.

2. Bryant Urstadt, Imagine There's no Oil: scenes from a liberal apocalypse," *Harpers*, (August 2006), 35.

3. Catherine Keller, "Women Against Wasting the World," in *Reweaving the World*, edited by Irene Diamond and Gloria Feman Orenstein (San Francisco: Sierra Club Books, 1990), 262.

4. Grace Halsell, *Prophecy and Politics* (Westport, CT: Lawrence Hall & Co., 1986), 67.

5. Charlene Spretnak, "The Christian Right's 'Holy War' Against Feminism," in *The Politics of Women's Spirituality* edited by Charlene Spretnak (Garden City, NY: Anchor Press/Doubleday, 1982), 488.

6. Catherine Keller, *God and Power* (Minneapolis: Fortress Press 2005), 37

7. James Ogilvy, *Many-Dimensional Man* (New York: Harper Colophon, 1979), 49.

8. See Michael Barkun, "Divided Apocalypse" Soundings, *An Interdisciplinary Journal* LXVI (Fall, 1983).

9. Northrop Frye, "Varieties of Literary Utopias," in *Utopias and Utopian Thought*, edited by F. E. Manuel (Boston: Beacon Press, 1957), 41.

10. Maynard Kaufman, "The New Homesteading Movement: From Utopia to Eutopia" in *The Family, Communes and Utopian Societies*, edited by Sallie TeSelle (New York: Harper Torchbooks, 1972).

11. See also Mircea Eliade, "Eschatology and Cosmogony," chapter 4 in *Myth and Reality* (New York: Harper Torchbooks, 1967), for more examples.

12. See E. S. Stavrianos, *The Promise of the Coming Dark Age* (San Francisco: W. H. Freeman & Company, 1976).

13. Leo Marx, *The Machine in the Garden* (Oxford: Oxford University Press, 1964), 127.

CHAPTER VII

1. Thomas Berry, *The Great Work* (New York: Bell Tower, 1999), 163.

2. *Ibid.*, 171-195.

3. Brian Swimme, *The Hidden Heart of the Cosmos* (Maryknoll, NY: Orbis Books, 1996), 19.

4. Charlene Spretnak, "Ecofeminism: Our Roots and Flowering," in *Reweaving the World* edited by Irene Diamond and Gloria Orenstein (San Francisco: Sierra Club Books, 1990), 8.

5. Judith Todd, "On Common Ground: Native American and Feminist Spirituality Approaches in the Struggle to Save Mother Earth," in *The Politics of Women's Spirituality*, edited by Charlene Spretnak (Garden City, NY: Anchor Books, 1982), 434.

6. Vandana Shiva, Staying Alive (London: Zed Books, 1988), 14.

7. Baba Copper, "The Voice of Women's Spirituality in Futurism," in *The Politics of Women's Spirituality*, edited by Charlene Spretnak, 500.

8. Catherine Keller, "Women Against Wasting the Earth," in *Reweaving the World*, edited by Diamond and Orenstein, 262.

9. Rosemary Radford Ruether, *Goddesses and the Divine Feminine* (Berkeley: University of California Press, 2005), 5, 289. See also Carol Christ, *Laughter of Aphrodite* (San Francisco: Harper and Row, 1987), Chapter 10, "Reclaiming Goddess History."

10. Charles Hartshorne, *Man's Vision of God* (Chicago: Willet, Clark & Co., 1941), 192, 200.

11. Alfred North Whitehead, *Process and Reality* (New York: The Humanities Press, 1957) 524.

12. John B. Cobb and David Ray Griffin, *Process Theology* (Philadelphia: Westminster Press, 1976), 135.

13. Paul Tillich, *Systematic Theology*, III (Chicago: University of Chicago Press, 1963), 290, 294.

14. Yves Congar, *I Believe in the Holy Spirit*, III (New York: Seabury Press, 1983), 206.

15. *Ibid.*, 219.

16. *Ibid.*, 144.

17. Quoted by Eleanor Rae and Bernice Marie-Daly, *Created in Her Image* (New York: Crossroads, 1990), 113.

18. Leonardo Boff and Phillip Berryman, *Cry of the Earth, Cry of the Poor* (Maryknoll, NY: Orbis Books, 1997), 158-173.

19. Eleanor Rae, *Woman, The Earth, The Divine* (Maryknoll, NY: Orbis Books, 1994) 90-93.
20. Mark I. Wallace, *Fragments of the Spirit* (New York: Continuum, 1996), 1
21. Rosemary Radford Ruether, *Goddesses and the Divine Feminine*, 297, 307.
22. *Wallace, Fragments of the Spirit*, 158.
23. Harvey Cox, *Fire from Heaven*. (Reading, PA.: Addison-Wesley Publishing, 1995, 245.
24. Robert Heilbronner, *An Inquiry into the Human Prospect* (New York: W. W. Norton & Co., 1975) 141.

CHAPTER VIII

1. D. H. Lawrence, quoted in Nancy Wood, editor, *The Serpent's Tongue*. (New York: Dutton Books, 1997), 56-57.
2. Carolyn Merchant, *The Death of Nature* (San Francisco: Harper & Row, 1980), 293.
3. Catherine Albanese, *Nature Religion in America* (Chicago: University of Chicago Press, 1990), 200.
4. John Michel, "The Ideal World View," in *The Schumacher Lectures*, edited by Satish Kumar (New York: Harper & Row, 1981), 113.
5. Mircea Eliade, *Cosmos and History* (New York: Harper Torchbooks, 1954), 9.
6. Peter Kropotkin, *Fields, Factories, and Workshops Tomorrow* (New York: Harper Torchbooks, 1975).
7. Eliade, *Cosmos and History*, 85-86.
8. Michel, "The Ideal World View," 114.
9. Eliade, *Cosmos and History*, 154.
10. Gordon Kaufman, *In Face of Mystery* (Cambridge: Harvard University Press: 1993), 131.
11. Donald Worster, *Nature's Economy* (Cambridge University Press, 2006), 28, 55, 81, 92, 109, 382.
12. See Richard Heinberg, *Memories and Visions of Paradise* (Los Angeles: Tarcher, 1989).
13. Chellis Glendenning, *My Name is Chellis and I'm In Recovery from Western Civilization* (Boston: Shambhala, 1994), 181.
14. *Ibid.*, 210.
15. Richard Rubenstein, *After Auschwitz* (Indianapolis: Bobbs-Merrill, 1966), 137.
16. Albert Camus, *The Myth of Sisyphus* (New York: Vintage Books, 1955), 113.
17. Matthew Fox, *Creation Spirituality* (San Francisco: Harper, 1991), 100.
18. Margot Adler, *Drawing Down The Moon* (Boston: Beacon Press, 1986), 24-25.
19. *Ibid.*, 20.
20. Starhawk, *The Earth Path* (San Francisco: Harper, 2004), 43.
21. Adler, *Drawing Down the Moon*, 381.

22. Erik Davis, *TechGnosis* (New York: Crown Publishers, 2004), 224.
23. Richard Heinberg, *Celebrate the Solstice* (Wheaton, IL: Quest Books, 1993), 138.
24. Ly de *Angeles* & Thomas van Dooren, editors, *Pagan Visions for a Sustainable Future* (Woodbury, MN: Llewllyn Publications, 2005).
25. Adler, *Drawing Down the Moon*, 418, 455.
26. Colin Mason, *The 2030 Spike* (London: Earthscan Publications, LTD., 2003), 167.
27. See Rosemary Radford Ruether, *Goddesses and the Divine Feminine* (Berkeley: University of California Press, 2005), 296.
28. Adler, *Drawing Down the Moon*, 413.
29. Rhiannon Ryall, *West Country Wicca: A Journal of the Old Religion* (Custer, WA: Phoenix Publishing Co., 1989), 4.
30. Adler, *Drawing Down the Moon*, 391.
31. James Lovelock, *The Ages of Gaia* (New York: W. W. Norton, 1995), 199.
32. Stephan Harding, *Animate Earth* (Foxhole, Dartington, Totnes, Devon: Green Books, 2006), 29.
33. Rosemary Radford Ruether, "Motherearth and the Megamachine: A Theology of Liberation in a Feminine, Somatic and Ecological Perspective," in *Womanspirit Rising*, edited by Carol Christ and Judith Plaskow (San Francisco: Harper & Row, 1979).
34. Leonardo Boff and Phillip Berryman, *Cry of the Earth, Cry of the Poor* (Maryknoll, NY: Orbis Books, 1997), 158-173.
35. Carol Christ, *Laughter of Aphrodite* (San Francisco: Harper & Row, 1987), 106-108.
36. Carol Christ, *Rebirth of the Goddess* (Reading, MA: Addison Wesley, 1997), 41, 146.
37. Carol Christ, *Laughter of Aphrodite*, 110
38. Demetra George, *Mysteries of the Dark Moon* (San Francisco: Harper, 1992), 62, 91.
39. See Judith Plaskow, The Coming of Lilith: Toward a Feminist Theology." in *Womanspirit Rising*, edited by Carol Christ and Judith Plaskow.
40. See Ake Hultkrantz, *Native Religions in North America* (Prospect Heights, IL: Waveland Press,1987), 27.
41. Charlene Spretnak, *States of Grace* (Harper San Francisco, 1991), 89.
42. Richard Heinberg, *A New Covenant with Nature* (Wheaton, IL: Quest Books, 1996), 147.
43. Clark Wissler, *Indians of the United States* (New York: Doubleday Anchor, 1940), 263-265.
44. Frank Waters, *The Book of the Hopi* (New York: Ballantine Books, 1963), 339.
45. See Andre Lopez, *Pagans in our Midst* (Rooseveltown, NY: Akwesasne Notes, nd).

46. Jerry Mander, *In the Absence of the Sacred* (San Francisco: Sierra Club Books, 1991), 215, 219.

47. *Ibid.*, 204.

48. Quoted by Carol Christ, in *Rebirth of the Goddess*, 114.

49. Joe Sanchez, quoted by Mander, *In the Absence of the Sacred*, 223.

50. Winona LaDuke, *Indigenous People, Power, and Politics: A Renewable Future for the Seventh Generation.* (Honor the Earth Publications, 2004).

51. Elizabeth Tooker, editor, *Native North American Spirituality of the Eastern Woodlands* (Macwah, NJ: Paulist Press, 1979), 18.

52. Mander, *In the Absence of the Sacred*, 191.

53. John G. Neihardt, *Black Elk Speaks* (Lincoln: University of Nebraska Press, 1961), 173.

54. *Ibid.*, 198.

55. Mander, *In the Absence of the Sacred*, 269.

56. Hultkrantz, *Native Religions in North America.*

57. Mander, *In The Absence of the Sacred*, 230-245.

58. Val Plumwood, "Place, Politics, and Spirituality," in *Pagan Visions for a Sustainable Future*, 233.

CHAPTER IX

1. Paul H. Ray and Sherry Ruth Anderson, *The Cultural Creatives* (New York: Three Rivers Press, 2000) 39, 191-193.

2. *Ibid.*, 33, 65-95.

3. Naomi Klein, *The Shock Doctrine: The Rise of Disaster Capitalism* (New York: Metropolitan Books, 2007), 444 and chapters 7 and 13.

4. *Ibid.*, 298.

5. David Ray Griffin, *Christian Faith and the Truth Behind 9/11* (Louisville, KY: Westminster John Knox Press, 2006) 137.

6. W. Jackson Davis, *The Seventh Year: Industrial Civilization in Transition.* (New York: W. W. Norton & Co., 1979. 282.

7. Howard T. And Elizabeth C. Odum, *A Prosperous Way Down* (University Press of Colorado, 2001), 270.

8. *Ibid.*, 86.

9. David Korten, *The Great Turning: From Empire to Earth Community* (San Francisco: Berrett-Koehler Publishers, 2006), 325.

10. Mark I. Wallace, *Fragments of the Spirit* (New York: Continuum, 1996), 212.

11. James Robertson, *The Sane Alternative* (St Paul: River Basin Publishing, 1978), 103-113.

12. Thom Hartmann, *Unequal Protection: The Rise of Corporate Dominion and the Theft of Human Rights* (Emmaus, PA: Rodale Books, 2002), 190.

13. Korten, *The Great Turning*, 333.

14. Hartmann, *Unequal Protection*, 279-298, 342.

15. Korten, *The Great Turning*, 353.

16. Anthony F. C. Wallace, "Revitalization Movements," *American Anthropologist*, 58 (1956), 267.

17. *Ibid.*, 269.

18. James Mooney, *The Ghost-Dance Religion* (Chicago: University of Chicago Press, 1965), 115-120.

19. See David Domke, *God Willing* (London and Ann Arbor: Pluto Press, 2004) and Kevin Phillips, *American Theocracy* (New York: Viking Penguin, 2006).

20. Anthony F. C. Wallace, *The Death and Rebirth of the Seneca* (New York: Vintage, 1972).

21. William G. McLaughlin, *Revivals, Awakenings, and Reform* (Chicago: University of Chicago Press, 1978). It is interesting to note that the new religious orientation McLaughlin expected was similar to that of the Culture Creatives of today, including "a new sense of the mystical unity of all mankind and of the vital harmony between man and nature . . . . The nourishing spirit of mother earth, not the wrath of an angry father above, will dominate religious thought." 214.

22. Dmitry Orlov, *Reinventing Collapse* (Gabriola Island, BC: New Society Publishers, 2008) 105.

BIBLIOGRAPHY

Adler, Margot, *Drawing Down the Moon*. Boston: Beacon Press, 1979, 1986.

Albanese, Catherine L., *Nature Religion in America*. Chicago: University of Chicago Press, 1990.

Angeles, Ly de, et. al., editors, *Pagan Visions for a Sustainable Future*. Woodbury, MN: Llewllyn Publications, 2005.

Bacevich, Andrew, *The New American Militarism*. New York: Oxford University Press, 2005

Bang, Jan Martin, *Ecovillages: A Practical Guide to Sustainable Communities*. Gabriola Island, BC.: New Society Publishers, 2005.

Barbour, Ian, (ed.), *Western Man and Environmental Ethics*. Reading, MA: Addison-Wesley Publishing Co. 1973.

Barnet, Richard J. *The Lean Years*. New York: Simon & Schuster, 1980.

Barney, Gerald O., *The Global 2000 Report to the President*. New York: Pergamon Press, 1980

Batchelor, John Calvin, *The Birth of the Peoples Republic of Antarctica*. New York: Dial, 1983

Bellah, Robert, et. al., *Habits of the Heart*. New York: Harper and Row, 1985.

Berdyaev, Nicholas, *Truth and Revelation*. New York: Collier Books, 1962.

Berger, John, *Pig Earth*. New York: Pantheon, 1979.

Berry, Thomas, *The Dream of the Earth*. San Francisco: Sierra Club Books, 1988.

Berry, Thomas, *The Great Work*. New York; Bell Tower, 1999.

Berry Wendell, *The Gift of Good Land*. San Francisco: North Point Press, 1981.

Berry, Wendell, *The Unsettling of America*. San Francisco, Sierra Club Books, 1977.

Boff, Leonardo, and Phillip Berryman, *Cry of the Earth; Cry of the Poor*. Maryknoll, NY: Orbis Books, 1997.

Brown, Lester, *Outgrowing the Earth*. New York: W. W. Norton, 2004.

Brown, Norman O. *Life Against Death: The Psychoanalytic Meaning of History*. New York; Vintage Books, 1959.

Burns, Scott, *Home, Inc.*, Garden City, New York: Doubleday& Company, 1975.

Campolo, Tony, *Speaking My Mind*. Nashville: W Publishing Group, 2004.

Campbell, Colin J., *The Coming Oil Crisis*. Brentwood, Essex, England: Multi-science Publications and Petroconsultants, 1997.

Camus, Albert, *The Myth of Sisyphus*. New York: n Vintage Books, 1955

Carson, Rachel, *Silent Spring*. New York: Crest Books, 1962.

Catton, William R. *Overshoot: The Ecological Basis of Revolutionary Change*. Urbana, IL: University of Illinois Press, 1980.

Christ, Carol P. *Laughter of Aphrodite*. San Francisco: Harper and Row, 1987

Christ, Carol P. *Rebirth of the Goddess*. Reading, MA: Addison Wesley, 1997.

Christ, Carol P. *She Who Changes: Re-imagining the Divine in the World*. New York: Palgrave Macmillan, 2003.

Christ, Carol P., (ed) *Womanspirit Rising*. San Francisco, Harper and Row, 1979.

Clark, William R., *Petrodollar Warfare*. New Society Publishers, 2005.

Clark, Wilson, *Energy for Survival: The Alternative to Extinction*. Anchor Books. 1975

Cobb, John, *Economics, Ecology and Justice*. Maryknoll, NY: Orbis, 1992.

Cobb, John B. and David Ray Griffin, *Process Theology*. Philadelphia: Westminster, 1976

Cobb, John B., et. al. *The American Empire and the Commonwealth of God*. Louisville, KY: Westminster John Knox Press, 2006.

Commoner, Barry, *The Closing Circle*. Bantam Books, 1972.

Commoner, Barry, *The Poverty of Power*. New York: Alfred A Knopf, 1976.

Congar, Yves, *I Believe in the Holy Spirit*. New York: Seabury Press, 1983.

Cox, Harvey, *The Feast of Fools*. Cambridge, MA.:Harvard University Press, 1969.

Cox, Harvey, *The Secular City*. New York: Macmillan, 1965.

Cox, Harvey, *Fire From Heaven*. Reading, PA: Addison-Wesley Publishing, 1995. Crossan, John Dominic, *Jesus: A Revolutionary Biography*. San Francisco: Harper, 1995.

Crossley, D.A., et. al., "The Positive Interactions in Ecosystems," *In Agricultural Ecosystems*, edited by R. Lowrance, et. al., New York: John Wiley, 1984.

Daly, Herman E. *Beyond Growth*. Boston: Beacon Press, 1996.

Daly, Herman E., Economics, *Ecology, Ethics: Essays Toward a Steady-State Economy*.

San Francisco: Wh. H. Freeman and Company, 1980

Daly, Herman E. and Cobb, John B., *For the Common Good*. Boston: Beacon Press, 1989

Daly, Herman E., and Joshua Farley, *Ecological Economics*. Washington DC: Island Press, 2004

Darley, Julian, *High Noon for Natural Gas: The New Energy Crisis*. White River Junction, Vermont: Chelsea Green Publishing Co., 2004

Davis, Erik, *TechGnosis*. New York; Crown Publishers, 1998, 2004.

Davis, W. Jackson, *The Seventh Year: Industrial Civilization in Transition*. New York: WW Norton, 1979.

Defeyes, Kenneth S., *Hubbert's Peak: The Impending World Oil Shortage*. Princeton University Press, 2001.

DeMoll, Lane, and Gigi Coe, (editors) *Stepping Stones*. New York: Schocken Books, 1978.

DeRomana, Alfredo L., *Post-Crisis Equilibrium: From Growth to Harmony*. Interculture, 104 and 105, Monchanin Cross-Cultural Centre.

Devall, Bill, Living *Richly in an Age of Limits*

Devall, Bill, and George Sessions, *Deep Ecology*. Salt Lake City: Peregrine Smith Books, 1985

Diamond, Irene, and Orenstein, Gloria, (editors), *Reweaving the World: The Emergence of Ecofeminism*. San Francisco: Sierra Books, 1990.

Diamond, Jared, *Collapse*. New York: Viking, 2005.

Domke, David, *God Willing?*. London and Ann Arbor: Pluto Press, 2004.

Donahue, Brian, *Reclaiming the Commons*. New Haven: Yale University Press, 1999.

Dubos, Rene, *A God Within*. New York: Charles Scribner's Sons, 1972

Duncan, Richard C., *The Peak of World Oil Production and the Road to Olduvai Gorge*.

Ehrlich, Paul and Anne, *The End of Affluence*. New York: Ballantine Books, 1974.

Eliade, Mircea, *Cosmos and History*. New York: Harper Torchbooks, 1954, 1959.

Eliade, Mircea, *Myth and Reality*. New York: Harper Torchbooks, 1967.

Eliade, Mircea, *Occultism, Witchcraft and Cultural Fashions*. Chicago: University of Chicago Press, 1976

Eliade, Mircea, *Patterns in Comparative Religion*. Cleveland, Ohio, Meridian Books, 1963.

Eliade, Mircea, *The Quest: History and Meaning in Religion*. Chicago: University of Chicago Press, 1969.

Fox, Matthew, *Creation Spirituality*. San Francisco: Harper, 1991.

Fox, Matthew, *The Coming of the Cosmic Christ*. San Francisco: Harper and Row, 1988.

Fox, Matthew, *Original Blessing*. Santa Fe: Bear and Company, 1983

Freeman, S. David, *Winning our Energy Independence*. Salt Lake City: Gibbs Smith, 2007.

Galloway, Allan D., *The Cosmic Christ*. London: Nisbet & Co., Ltd., 1951.

George, Demetra, *Mysteries of the Dark Moon*. San Francisco: Harper, 1992.

Gever, John, et. al., *Beyond Oil*. Cambridge, MA, Ballinger Publishing Co.,1986.

Glendinning, Chellis, *My Name is Chellis & I'm in Recovery From Western Civilization*. Boston: Shambhala, 1994.

Greco, Thomas H., Jr., *New Money for Healthy Communities*. Tuscon, AZ, by author, 1994

Griffin, David Ray, *Christian Faith and the Truth Behind 9/11*. Louisville, KY: Westminster John Knox Press, 2006.

Griffin, David Ray, *The New Pearl Harbor*. Northampton, MA: Interlink, 2004.

Griffin, Susan, *Woman and Nature*. New York: Harper and Row, 1978.

Halsell, Grace, *Prophecy and Politics*. Westport CT: Lawrence Hall & Co. 1986.

Harding, Stephan, *Animate Earth*. Foxhole, Dartington, Totnes, Devon, Green Books, 2006

Harris, Sam, *The End of Faith*. New York: W. W. Norton, 2005.

Hartmann, Thom, *The Last Hours of Ancient Sunlight*. New York; Three Rivers Press, 2004.

Hartmann, Thom, *Unequal Protection*. Emmaus, :PA: Rodale Books, 2002.

Hartshorne, Charles, *Man's Vision of God*. Chicago: Willet, Clark & Company, 1941.

Hayden, Tom, *The Lost Gospel of the Earth*. San Francisco, Sierra Club Books, 1996.

Hayes, Dennis, *Rays of Hope: The Transition to a Post Petroleum World*. New York; W.W. Norton, 1977.

Heilbroner, Robert, *An Inquiry into The Human Prospect*. New York: W.W. Norton, 1975.

Heinberg, Richard, *Celebrate the Solstice*. Wheaton, IL: Quest Books, 1993.

Heinberg, Richard, *A New Covenant with Nature*. Wheaton, IL: Quest Books, 1996.

Heinberg, Richard, *Memories and Visions of Paradise*. Los Angeles: Tarcher, 1989.

Heinberg, Richard, *The Oil Depletion Protocol*. New Society Publishers, 2006.

Heinberg, Richard., *The Party's Over*. New Society Publishers, 2005.

Heinberg, Richard., *Powerdown: Options and Actions for a Post Carbon World*. New Society Publishers, 2004.

Hendricks, Obery M, Jr., *The Politics of Jesus*. New York: Doubleday, 2006.

Horsley, Richard, *Jesus and Empire*. Louisville, KY: Westminster John Knox Press, 2004.

Hultkrantz, Ake, *Native Religions of North America*. Prospect Heights, IL: Waveland Press, 1987.

Illich, Ivan, *Deschooling Society*. New York: Harper, 1970.

Illich, Ivan, *Medical Nemesis*. New York: Pantheon Books, 1976.

Illich, Ivan, *Shadow Work*. Boston: Marion Boyers, 1986.

Illich, Ivan, Tools for Conviviality. New York: Harper and Row, 1973.

Illich, Ivan, *Toward a History of Needs*. New York: Pantheon Books, 1978.

Jackson, Wes, *Altars of Unhewn Stone*. San Francisco: North Point Press, 1987.

Johnson, Chalmers, *The Sorrows of Empire*. New York: Metropolitan Books, 2004

Johnson, Warren and Hardesty, John, editors, *Economic Growth Vs. the Environment*. Wadsworth Publishing Co., 1971.

Johnson, Warren, *Muddling Toward Frugality.*, Boulder, CO, Shambhala, 1979.

Kaufman, Gordon, *In Face of Mystery*. Cambridge, Harvard University Press, 1993.

Kaufman, Maynard, "Faustian Striving and the Gnostic Dimension in Western Civilization, Society For Utopian Studies, edited by Edward D. Wilson, nd.

Kaufman, Maynard, "From Domination to Cooperation: Ethical and Economic Motivations Toward Sustainable Food Production Systems" in Allen, Patricia and Van Dusen, Debra (editors), *Global Perspectives on Agroecology and Sustainable Agricultural Systems*. Santa Cruz: University of California, 1988.

Kaufman, Maynard, "Post-Christian Aspects of the Radical Theology" in Altizer, Thomas J. J., (ed), *Toward a New Christianity: Readings in the Death of God Theology*. New York: Harcourt, Brace and World, 1967.

Kaufman, Maynard, "The New Homesteading Movement: From Utopia to Eutopia" in Sallie TeSelle, (ed), *The Family, Communes and Utopian Societies*. Harper Torchbooks, 1971.

Keller, Catherine, *Apocalypse Now and Then*. Boston: Beacon Press, 1996.

Keller, Catherine, *God and Power*. Minneapolis: Fortress Press, 2005.

Kennedy, Margrit, *Interest and Inflation Free Money*. Okemos, MI: Seva International, 1995.

Kimbrell, Andrew, *The Human Body Shop*. San Francisco: Harper, 1993.

Kingsolver, Barbara, *Animal, Vegetable, Miracle*. New York: Harper Collins, 2007.

Klare, Michael T., *Blood and Oil*. New York: Henry Holt, 2004.

Klare, Michael T., *Resource War*s. New York: Henry Holt & Co. 2001.

Klein, Naomi, *The Shock Doctrine*. New York: Metropolitan Books, 2007.

Kolbert, Elizabeth, *Field Notes from a Catastrophe*. New York: Bloomsbury Publishing, 2006.

Korten, David C., *The Great Turning*. San Francisco: Berrett-Koehler Publishers, and Hartford, CT: Kumarian Press, 2006.

Korten, David C., *The Post-Corporate World: Life After Capitalism*. San Francisco: Berrett—Koehler Publishers and Hartford, CT: KumarianPress1999.

Korten, David, *When Corporations Rule the World*. San Francisco: Berrett-Koehler P:ublishers and Hartford, CT: Kumarian Press, 1995.

Kropotkin, Peter, *Fields, Factories and Workshops Tomorrow*. New York: Harper Torch books, 1975.

Kumar, Satish, (ed) *The Schumacher Lectures*, New York: Harper and Row, 1981.

Kunstler, James Howard, *The Long Emergency*. New York: 2004.

Lerner, Michael, *The Left Hand of God*. San Francisco: Harper, 2006.

LaDuke, Winona, *Indigenous Peoples, Power & Politics*. Honor the Earth Publications, 2004

Lewis, R.W.B., *The American Adam*. Chicago, University of Chicago Press, 1955.

Lietaer, Bernard, *The Future of Money*. London: Century, 2001.

Lindsey, Hal, *The Late Great Planet Earth*. Grand Rapids, Zondervan, 1970.

Lipset, Seymour Martin, *American Exceptionalism*. New York: W.W. Norton, 1996.

Lobell, John, *The Little Green Book*. Boulder, CO, Shambhala, 1981.

Lopez, Andre, *Pagans in Our Midst*. Rooseveltown NY: Akwesasne Notes, nd.

Lovelock, James, *The Ages of Gaia*. New York: W. W. Norton, 1988, 1995.

Lovelock, James, *Gaia, A New Look at Life on Earth*. Oxford University Press, 1979, 2000.

Lovins, Amory, *Soft Energy Paths*. New York: Harper Colophon Books, 1979.

Lovins, Amory, et. al., *Winning the Oil Endgame.* Rocky Mountain Institute, 2004.

Lowith, Karl, *Meaning in History.* University of Chicago Press, 1949,1957

Lucas, George R, and Thomas W. Ogletree, *Lifeboat Ethics: The Moral Dilemmas of World Hunger.* New York: Harper Forum Books, 1976.

Mander, Jerry, Four *Arguments for the Elimination of Television.* Morrow Quill, 1978

Mander, Jerry, *In the Absence of the Sacred.* San Francisco, Sierra Books, 1991.

Manuel, F. E., (ed.), *Utopias and Utopian Thought.* Boston: Beacon P:ress, 1957.

Marx, Leo, *The Machine in the Garden.* Oxford: Oxford University Press, 1964.

Mason, Colin, *The 2030 Spike.* London: Earthscan Publications, Ltd., 2003.

McFague, Sallie, *The Body of God.* Minneapolis: Fortress Press, 1993.

McLaughlin, William G. *Revivals, Awakenings and Reform.* Chicago: University of Chicago Press, 1978.

Meadows, Donella, et. al., *The Limits to Growth.* New York: University Books, 1972.

Meadows, Donella, et. al., *Beyond the Limits.* Chelsea Green Publishing Co., 1992

Meadows, Donella, et. al., *Limits to Growth: The Thirty Update.* Chelsea Green, 2004

Merchant, Carolyn, *Earthcare: Women and the Environment.* New York: Routledge, 1995.

Merchant, Carolyn, *The Death of Nature.* San Francisco: Harper and Row, 1980.

Mesarovic, Mihaljlo and Pestel, Eduard, *Mankind at the Turning Point*. Signet Books, 1974.

Mills, Stephanie, *Epicurean Simplicity*. Washington: Island Press, 2002

Mooney, James, *The Ghost-Dance Religion*. Chicago: University of Chicago Press, 1965.

Mumford, Lewis, *The Myth of the Machine*: The Pentagon of Power. New York: Harcourt, Brace Jovanovich, 1970.

Mumford, Lewis, *Technics and Civilization*. Harbinger books, 1963.

Neihardt, John G., *Black Elk Speaks*. Lincoln: University Of Nebraska Press, 1961.

Noble, David, *The Religion of Technology*. New York: Alfred A. Knopf, 1998. Nordhaus, Ted, and Michael Shellenberger, *Break Through*. (Boston: Houghton Mifflin Company, 2007.

Odum, Howard T., *Environment Power and Society*. Wiley Interscience, 1971.

Odum, Howard T. and Odum, Elizabeth C., *A Prosperous Way Down*, University Press of Colorado, 2001.

Ogilvy, James, *Many-Dimensional Man*. New York: Harper Colophon, 1979.

Olkowski, Helga, et. al., *The Integral Urban House*. San Francisco, Sierra Club Books, 1979.

Ophuls, William, and Boyan, Stephen, *Ecology and the Politics of Scarcity Revisited, The Unraveling of the American Dream*. New York: W. H. Freeman & Co., 1992.

Orlov, Dmitry, *Reinventing Collapse*. Gabriola Island, BC: New Society Publishers: 2008.

Orr, David, *Earth in Mind*. Washington, DC: Island Press, 1994.

Pfeiffer, Dale Allen, *Eating Fossil Fuels*. New Society Publishers, 2006.

Phillips, Kevin, *American Theocracy*. New York: Viking Penguin, 2006.

Pimentel, David and Marcia, *Food, Energy and Society*. New York: John Wiley, 1996.

Plant, Judith, editor, *Healing the Wounds, The Promise of Ecofeminism*. Philadelphia and Santa Cruz: New Society Publishers, 1989.

Polanyi, Karl, *The Great Transformation*. Boston: Beacon Press, 1944, 1957.

Pollan, Michael, *The Omnivore's Dilemma*. New York: Penguin Press, 2006.

Pyle, George, *Raising Less Corn, More Hell*. New York: Public Affairs, 2005.

Rae, Eleanor, *Women, The Earth, The Divine*. Maryknoll, NY: Orbis Books, 1994.

Rae, Eleanor, and Bernice Marie-Daly, *Created in Her Image*. New York: Crossroad 1990.

Ray, Ray, Paul H., and Sherry Ruth Anderson, *The Cultural Creatives*. New York: Three Rivers Press, 2000.

Richards, Michael, *Sustainable Operating Systems: The Post Petrol Paradigm*. Cedar Rapids, IA Innovation Press, 2006.

Renshaw, Edward F., *The End of Progress*. Duxbury Press, 1976.

Rifkin, Jeremy, *Entropy*. New York: Viking P:res, 1980

Robertson, James, *Future Wealth*. New York: Bootstrap Press, 1990.

Robertson, James, *Future Work*. New York: Universe Books, 1985.

Robertson, James, *The Sane Alternative*. St. Paul: River Basin Publishing, 1978.

Rubenstein, Richard, *After Auschwitz*. Indianapolis: Bobbs-Merrill1966

Ruether, Rosemary Radford, and Dieter Hessel, editors, *Christianity and Ecology*. Cambridge: Harvard University Press, 2000.

Ruether, Rosemary Radford, *God and Gaia*. Harper San Francisco, 1992

Ruether, Rosemary Radford, *Goddesses and the Divine Feminine*. Berkeley: U. of Cal. Press 2005.

Reuther, Rosemary Radford, *New Woman New Earth*. New York; Seabury Press, 1975.

Ruppert, Michael, *Crossing the Rubicon: The Decline of the American Empire at the End of the Age of Oil*. Gabriola Island: New Society Publishers, 2004.

Ryall, Rhiannon, *West Country Wicca*. Phoenix Publishing Co., 1989.

Sale, Kirkpatrick, *Dwellers in the Land*. Philadelphia: New Society Press, 1991.

Sale, Kirkpatrick, *Human Scale*. G. P. Putnam's Pedigree Books, 1980.

Savinar, Matt, *The Oil Age is Over*. Kearney, NE: Morris Publishing, 2005

Schumacher, E. F., *Small is Beautiful*. New York: Harper Torchbooks, 1973.

Shiva, Vandana, *Staying Alive: Women, Ecology and Development*. London: Zed Books, 1988.

Simmons, Matthew R., *Twilight in the Desert*. John Wiley & Sons, 2005.

Sleeth, J. Matthew, *Serve God, Save the Planet*. Chelsea Green Publishing, 2006.

Spretnak, Charlene, *States of Grace*. Harper San Francisco, 1991.

Spretnak, Charlene, *Missing Mary*. New York: Macmillan Palgreave, 2004

Spretnak, Charlene, (ed), *The Politics of Women's Spirituality*. Doubleday Anchor Books, 1982.

Spretnak, Charlene, *The Spiritual Dimension of Green Politics*. Santa Fe: Bear & Co., 1986.

Starhawk, *Dreaming the Dark*. Boston: Beacon Press, 1982.

Starhawk, *The Earth Path*. San Francisco, Harper, 2004

Starhawk, *The Spiral Dance*. San Francisco: Harper, 1979.

Stavrianos, L. S. *The Promise of the Coming Dark Age*. San Francisco, W. H. Freeman, 1976.

Strahan, David, *The Last Oil Shock*. United Kingdom, John Murray, 2007.

Stivers, Robert L. *The Sustainable Society: Ethics and Economic Growth*. Philadelphia: The Westminster Press, 1976.

Stobaugh, Robert, and Yergin, Daniel, editors, *Energy Future*. Ballantine Books, 1979.

Swimme, Brian, *The Hidden Heart of the Cosmos*. Maryknoll, NY, Orbis, 1996.

Swimme, Brian, *The Universe is a Green Dragon*. Santa Fe: Bear and Co., 1984.

Tainter, Joseph A. *The Collapse of Complex Societies*. Cambridge University Press, 1990.

Tertzakian, Peter, *A Thousand Barrels a Second*. New York: McGraw Hill, 2006.

Tillich, Paul, *Systematic Theology, Volume III*. Chicago: University of Chicago Press, 1963.

Tillich, Paul, *Theology of Culture*. New York: Galaxy Books, 1964.

Tombari, Carol Sue, *Power of the People*. Golden, CO: Fulcrum, 2008.

Tooker, Elizabeth, *Native North American Spirituality of the Eastern Woodlands*. Macwah, NJ: Paulist Press, 1979.

Urstadt, Bryant, "Imagine There's No Oil", *Harper's Magazine*, {August 2006) 31-40.

Wachtel, Paul L., *The Poverty of Affluence*, Philadelphia: New Society Publishers, 1989.

Wallace, Anthony F.C., "Revitalization Movements," *American Anthropologist*, Vol.58 (1956).

Wallace, Anthony F.C., *The Death and Rebirth of the Seneca*. New York: Vintage, 1972.

Wallace, Mark I. *Fragments of the Spirit*. New York: Continuum, 1996.

Wallis, Jim, *God's Politics*. San Francisco, Harper, 2005.

Waters, Frank, *The Book of the Hopi*. New York: Ballantine Books, 1963.

Weber, Max, *The Protestant Ethic and the Spirit of Capitalism*. New York: Charles Scribner's Sons, 1958.

Whitehead, Alfred North, *Process and Reality*. New York: Humanities Press, 1957.

Wilkinson, Loren, *Earthkeeping*. Grand Rapids: Eerdmans, 1980.

Wink, Walter, *Engaging The Powers*. Minneapolis: Fortress Press, 1992.

Wirzba, Norman, (ed), *The Essential Agrarian Reader*. Lexington: University of Kentucky Press, 2003.

Wissler, Clark, *Indians of the United States*. Doubleday Anchor, 1940, 1965.

Wood, Nancy, *The Serpent's Tongue*. New York: Dutton Books, 1977.

Worster, Donald, *Nature's Economy*. Cambridge University Press, 1985, 2006.

Yergin, Daniel, *The Prize*. New York: Simon & Schuster, 1991.

Zinn, Howard, *A People's History of the United States, 1492-Present*. New York: Harper, 1999